Bienvenu!

Just Enough **French**

D. L. Ellis, F. Clark

Pronunciation **Dr. J. Baldwin**

PASSPORT BOOKS
a division of *NTC Publishing Group*
Lincolnwood, Illinois USA

The publishers would like to thank the French Tourist
Office for their help during the preparation of this book

1990 Printing

This edition first published in 1983 by Passport Books,
a division of NTC Publishing Group,
4255 West Touhy Avenue,
Lincolnwood (Chicago), Illinois 60646-1975 U.S.A.
Originally published by Pan Books, © D.L. Ellis and
F. Clarke, 1981. All rights reserved. No part of this book may
be reproduced, stored in a retrieval system, or transmitted
in any form, or by any means, electronic, mechanical,
photocopying or otherwise, without the prior permission
of NTC Publishing Group.
Manufactured in the United States of America.

9 0 RD 9 8 7

Contents

Using the phrase book

- This phrase book is designed to help you get by in French-speaking countries, to get what you want or need. It concentrates on the simplest but most effective way you can express these needs in an unfamiliar language.
- The CONTENTS on p. 5 give you a good idea of which section to consult for the phrase you need.
- The INDEX on p. 151 gives more detailed information about where to look for your phrase.
- When you have found the right page you will be given:

  either — the exact phrase

  or — help in making up a suitable sentence

  and — help to get the pronunciation right
- The English sentences in **bold type** will be useful for you in a variety of different situations, so they are worth learning by heart. (See also DO IT YOURSELF, p. 142.)
- Wherever possible you will find help in understanding what French-speaking people say to *you*, in reply to your questions.
- If you want to practise the basic nuts and bolts of the language further, look at the DO IT YOURSELF section starting on p. 142.
- Note especially these three sections:

  Everyday expressions p. 11

  Shop talk p. 54

  Public notices p. 121

  You are sure to want to refer to them most frequently.
- When you arrive in a French-speaking country, make good use of the tourist information offices (see p. 23).

  North American addresses:

  French Government Tourist Office
  610 Fifth Avenue
  New York, NY 10020
  (212) 757-1125

  Quebec House
  17 West 50th Street
  New York, NY 10020
  (212) 397-0200

A note on the pronunciation system

In traveler's phrase books there is usually a pronunciation section which tries to teach English-speaking tourists how to correctly pronounce the language of the country they are visiting. This is based on the belief that in order to be understood, the speaker must have an accurate, authentic accent—that he must pronounce every last word letter-perfectly.

The authors of this book, on the other hand, wanted to devise a workable and usable pronunciation system. So they had to face the fact it is absolutely impossible for an average speaker of English who has no technical training in phonetics and phonetic transcription systems (which includes 98% of all the users of this book!) to reproduce the sounds of a foreign language with perfect accuracy, just from reading a phonetic transcription, cold—no prior background in the language. We also believe that you don't have to have perfect pronunciation in order to make yourself understood in a foreign country. After all, natives you run into will take into account that you are foreigners, and visitors, and more than likely they will feel gratified by your efforts to communicate and will probably go out of their way to try to understand you. They may even help you, and correct you, in a friendly manner. We have found, also, that visitors to a foreign country are not usually concerned with perfect pronunciation—they just want to get their message across, to communicate!

With this in mind, we have designed a pronunciation system which is of the utmost simplicity to use. This system does not attempt to give an accurate—but also problematical and tedious—representation of the sound system of the language, but instead uses common sound and letter combinations in English which are the closest to the sounds in the foreign language. In this way, the sentences transcribed for pronunciation should be read as naturally as possible, as if they were ordinary English. In no way does the user have to attempt to make the words sound "foreign." So, while to yourselves you will sound as if you are speaking ordinary English—or at least making ordinary English sounds—you will at the same time be making yourselves understood in another language. And, as the saying goes, practice makes perfect, so it is probably a good idea to repeat aloud to yourselves several times the phrases you think you are going to use, before you actually use them. This will give you greater confidence, and will also help in making yourself understood.

In French it is important to read each syllable with equal emphasis. For instance, in the following English example we have ten syllables and ten stresses: *Little Jack Horner sat in the corner*. Though this will probably sound rather mechanical to an English ear, it will help the French speaker to understand you.

Of course you may enjoy trying to pronounce a foreign language as well as possible and the present system is a good way to start. However, since it uses only the sounds of English, you will very soon need to depart from it as you imitate the sounds you hear the native speaker produce and to relate them to the spelling of the other language. Be prepared, however, for the relationship between pronunciation and spelling to be a complex one.

Bon courage!

Everyday expressions

[See also 'Shop talk' p. 54]

Hello	**Bonjour**
Good morning	bonshoor
Good day	**Salut** (friends only)
Good afternoon	saloo
Good evening	**Bonsoir**
	bonswah
Good night	**Bonne nuit**
	bon nwee
Goodbye	**Au revoir**
	o-revwah
See you later	**A tout à l'heure**
	ah tootahler
Yes	**Oui**
	wee
Please	**S'il vous plaît**
	sil voo pleh
Yes, please	**Oui, s'il vous plaît**
	wee sil voo pleh
Great!	**Formidable!**
	for-mee-dab
Thank you	**Merci**
	mair-see
Thank you very much	**Merci beaucoup**
	mair-see bo-coo
That's right	**C'est exact**
	set exah
No	**Non**
	non
No, thank you	**Non, merci**
	non mair-see
('Merci' by itself can also mean 'No thank you.')	
I disagree	**Je ne suis pas d'accord**
	sher ner swee pah dah-cor
Excuse me	**Pardon**
Sorry	par-don
Don't mention it	**De rien**
That's OK	der ree-an

That's good ⎤ I like it ⎦	**Ça va** sah vah
That's no good ⎤ I don't like it ⎦	**Ça ne va pas** sah ner vah pah
I know	**Je sais** sher seh
I don't know	**Je ne sais pas** sher ner seh pah
It doesn't matter	**Ça ne fait rien** sah ner feh ree-an
Where's the toilet, please?	**Où sont les WC, s'il vous plaît?** oo son leh veh-seh sil voo pleh
How much is that? [*point*]	**C'est combien, ça?** seh combee-an sah
Is the service included?	**Est-ce que le service est compris?** esk ler sairvees eh compree
Do you speak English?	**Parlez-vous anglais?** parleh-voo ahngleh
I'm sorry ...	**Je regrette ...** sher rer-gret ...
I don't speak French	**je ne parle pas français** sher ner parl pah frahn-seh
I only speak a little French	**je parle très peu le français** sher parl treh per ler frahn-seh
I don't understand	**je ne comprends pas** sher ner comprahn pah
Please can you ...	**S'il vous plaît, pouvez-vous ...** sil voo pleh pooveh-voo ...
repeat that?	**répéter?** reh-peh-teh
speak more slowly?	**parler plus lentement?** parleh ploo lahnt-mahn
write it down?	**l'écrire?** leh-creer
What is this called in French? [*point*]	**Comment ça s'appelle en français?** commahn sah sappel ahn frahn-seh

Crossing the border

ESSENTIAL INFORMATION

- Don't waste time just before you leave rehearsing what you're going to say to the border officials—the chances are that you won't have to say anything at all, especially if you travel by air.
- It's more useful to check that you have your documents handy for the journey: passport, tickets, money, travellers' checks, insurance documents, driving licence and car registration documents.
- Look out for these signs:
  DOUANE (customs)
  FRONTIÈRE (border)
  [*For futher signs and notices, see p. 121*]
- You may be asked routine questions by the customs officials [*see below*]. If you have to give personal details see 'Meeting people', p. 14. The other important answer to know is 'Nothing': **Rien** (ree-an)

ROUTINE QUESTIONS

Passport?	**Passeport?** passpor
Insurance?	**Assurance?** assoo-rahns
Registration document? (logbook)	**Carte grise?** cart greez
Ticket, please	**Billet, s'il vous plaît** bee-yeh sil voo pleh
Have you anything to declare?	**Avez-vous quelque chose à déclarer?** ahveh-voo kelk shoz ah deh-clah-reh
Where are you going?	**Où allez-vous?** oo alleh-voo
How long are you staying?	**Combien de temps comptez-vous rester?** combee-an der tahn conteh-voo resteh
Where have you come from?	**D'où venez-vous?** doo ver-neh voo

You may also have to fill in forms which ask for:

surname	**nom**
first name	**prénom**
maiden name	**nom de jeune fille**
date of birth	**date de naissance**
place of birth	**lieu de naissance**
address	**adresse**
nationality	**nationalité**
profession	**profession**
passport number	**numéro du passeport**
issued at	**fait à**
signature	**signature**

Meeting People

[*See also 'Everyday expressions', p. 11.*]

Breaking the ice

Hello ⎤
Good morning ⎦   **Bonjour (Salut)**
bonshoor (saloo)
(The above bracketed expression should only be used with people you know well.)

How are you?	**Ça va?**
	sah vah
Pleased to meet you	**Enchanté/e**
	ahn-shahn-teh
I am here ...	**Je suis ici ...**
	sher swee ee-see ...
on holiday	**en vacances**
	ahn vahcahns
on business	**pour affaires**
	poor affair
Can I offer you ...	**Puis-je vous offrir ...**
	pweesh vooz offreer ...
a drink?	**un verre?**
	an vair
a cigarette?	**une cigarette?**
	oon cigarette

a cigar?	**un cigare?**
	an cigar
Are you staying long?	**Vous êtes ici pour longtemps*?**
	voozet ee-see poor longtahn

Name

What is your name?	**Comment vous appelez-vous?**
	commahn vooz appleh-voo
My name is ...	**Je m'appelle ...**
	shmappel ...

Family

Are you married?	**Vous êtes marié/e*?**
	voozet maree-eh
I am ...	**Je suis ...**
	sher swee ...
married	**marié/e***
	maree-eh
single	**célibataire**
	cehlee-batair
This is ...	**Voici ...**
	vwah-see ...
my wife	**ma femme**
	mah fam
my husband	**mon mari**
	mon maree
my daughter	**ma fille**
	mah fee
my son	**mon fils**
	mon feess
my (boy) friend	**mon ami**
	mon-ahmee
my (girl) friend	**mon amie**
	mon-ahmee
my (male) colleague	**mon collègue**
	mon colleg
my (female) colleague	**ma collègue**
	mah colleg

* Use the first alternative for men, the second for women.

Do you have any children?	**Avez-vous des enfants?** ahveh-voo dez-ahnfahn
I have ...	**J'ai ...** sheh ...
one daughter	**une fille** oon fee
one son	**un fils** an feess
two daughters	**deux filles** der fee
three sons	**trois fils** trwah feess
No, I haven't any children	**Non je n'ai pas d'enfants** non sher neh pah dahnfahn

Where you live

Are you ...	**Vous êtes ...** voozet ...
Belgian?	**belge?** belsh
French?	**français/e?*** frahn-seh/-sez
from Luxembourg?	**du Luxembourg?** doo look-sahn-boor
Swiss?	**suisse?** sweess
I am ...	**Je suis ...** sher swee ...
American	**américain/e*** american/-ken
English	**anglais/e*** angleh/-glez

[*For other nationalities, see p. 134.*]

I live ...	**J'habite ...** shahbeet ...
in London	**Londres** lond
in England	**l'Angleterre** lahng-tair

* Use the first alternative for men, the second for women.

in the north	**dans le nord**
	dahn ler nor
in the south	**dans le sud**
	dahn ler sood
in the east	**dans l'est**
	dahn lest
in the west	**dans l'ouest**
	dahn looest
in the centre	**dans le centre**
	dahn ler sahnt

[For other countries, see p. 134.]

For the businessman and woman

I'm from . . . (firm's name)	**Je travaille pour . . .**
	sher trah-vy poor . . .
I have an appointment with . . .	**J'ai rendez-vous avec . . .**
	sheh rahndeh-voo ahvec . . .
May I speak to . . . ?	**Puis-je parler à . . . ?**
	pweesh parleh ah . . .
This is my card	**Voici ma carte**
	vwah-see mah cart
I'm sorry I'm late	**Je m'excuse d'être en retard**
	sher mexcooz det ahn rer-tar
Can I fix another appointment?	**Puis-je prendre un autre rendez-vous?**
	pweesh prahnd an ot rahndeh-voo
I'm staying at the (Paris) hotel	**Je suis à l'hôtel (Paris)**
	sher swee a lotel (pahree)
I'm staying in (St John's) road	**Je suis dans la rue (St Jean)**
	sher swee dahn lah roo (san-shahn)

Asking the way

ESSENTIAL INFORMATION

● Keep a look out for all these place names as you will find them on shops, maps and notices.

WHAT TO SAY

Excuse me, please	**Pardonnez-moi, s'il vous plaît** par-do-neh mwah sil voo pleh
How do I get ...	**Pour aller ...** poor alleh ...
to Paris?	**à Paris?** ah pahree
to rue St Pierre?	**à la rue Saint-Pierre?** ah lah roo san-pee-air
to the hotel Metropole?	**à l'hôtel Métropole?** ah lotel meh-tro-pol
to the airport?	**à l'aéroport?** ah lah-eh-ropor
to the beach?	**à la plage?** ah lah plash
to the bus station?	**à la gare d'autobus?** ah lah gar dotoboos
to the historic site?	**au site historique?** o seet eestoreek
to the market?	**au maché?** o marsheh
to the police station?	**au commissariat?** o commissaree-ah
to the port?	**au port?** o por
to the post office?	**à la poste?** ah lah post
to the railway station?	**à la gare?** ah lah gar
to the sports stadium?	**au stade?** o stad

to the tourist information office?	**au syndicat d'initiative?**
	o sandeecah dinisee-ativ
to the town centre?	**au centre de la ville?**
	o sahnt der lah veel
to the town hall?	**à la mairie?**
	ah lah mai-ree
Excuse me, please	**Pardonnez-moi, s'il vous plaît**
	par-do-neh mwah sil voo pleh
Is there . . . near by?	**Est-ce qu'il y a . . . près d'ici?**
	eskil yah . . . preh dee-see
an art gallery	**un musée d'art**
	an moozeh dar
a baker's	**une boulangerie**
	oon boolahn-shree
a bank	**une banque**
	oon bahnk
a bar	**un bar**
	an bar
a botanical garden	**un jardin botanique**
	an shardan botah-neek
a bus stop	**un arrêt d'autobus**
	an ahreh dotoboos
a butcher's	**une boucherie**
	oon booshree
a café	**un café**
	an cahfeh
a cake shop	**une pâtisserie**
	oon pahteess-ree
a campsite	**un camping**
	an camping
a car park	**un parking**
	an parking
a change bureau	**un bureau de change**
	an buro der shahnsh
a chemist's	**une pharmacie**
	oon pharmacy
a church	**une église**
	oon eh-gleez
a cinema	**un cinéma**
	an cinema
a delicatessen	**une charcuterie**
	oon sharcootree

Is there . . . near by?	Est-ce qu'il y a . . . près d'ici?
	eskil yah . . . preh dee-see
a dentist's	**un dentiste**
	an dahnteest
a department store	**un grand magasin**
	an grahn mahgahzan
a disco	**une discothèque**
	oon discotek
a doctor's surgery	**un docteur**
	an doc-ter
a dry cleaner's	**un pressing**
	an pressing
a fishmonger's	**une poissonnerie**
	oon pwah-son-ree
a garage (for repairs)	**un garage**
	an gahrash
a hairdresser's	**un coiffeur**
	an kwah-fer
a greengrocer's	**un marchand de légumes**
	an marshahn der lehgoom
a grocer's	**une épicerie**
	oon ehpeess-ree
a hardware shop	**une quincaillerie**
	oon kan-kay-ree
a Health and Social Security Office	**un bureau de la Sécurité Sociale**
	an buro der lah sehcooreeteh sossee-al
a hospital	**un hôpital**
	an opeetal
a hotel	**un hôtel**
	an otel
a hypermarket	**un hypermarché**
	an eepair-marsheh
a laundry	**une laverie**
	oon lav-ree
a museum	**un musée**
	an moo-zeh
a newsagent's	**un marchand de journaux**
	an marshahn der shoorno
a night club	**une boîte de nuit**
	oon bwaht der nwee
a petrol station	**une station service**
	oon stah-see-on sairvees

a post box	**une boîte à lettres**
	oon bwaht ah let
a public garden (town park)	**un jardin public**
	an shardan poobleek
a public telephone	**un téléphone**
	an telefon
a public toilet	**des WC publics**
	deh veh-seh poobleek
a restaurant	**un restaurant**
	an restorahn
a snack bar	**un snack**
	an snack
a sports ground	**un terrain de sport**
	an terran der spor
a supermarket	**un supermarché**
	an soopair-marsheh
a sweet shop	**une confiserie**
	oon confeez-ree
a swimming pool	**une piscine**
	oon pee-seen
a taxi stand	**une station de taxis**
	oon stah-see-on der taxee
a theatre	**un théâtre**
	an teh-aht
a tobacconist's	**un bureau de tabac**
	an buro der tahbah
a travel agent's	**une agence de voyage**
	oon ashahns der vwah-yash
a youth hostel	**une auberge de jeunesse**
	oon obairsh der sher-ness
a zoo	**un zoo**
	an zo-o

DIRECTIONS

- Asking where a place is, or if a place is nearby, is one thing; making sense of the answer is another.
- Here are some of the most important key directions and replies.

Left	**Gauche**
	goshe
Right	**Droite**
	drwaht

Straight on	**Tout droit** too drwah
There	**Là** lah
First left/right	**La première rue à gauche/droite** lah prem-yair roo ah goshe/drwaht
Second left/right	**La deuxième rue à gauche/droite** lah der-zee-em roo ah goshe/drwaht
At the crossroads	**Au carrefour** o carfoor
At the traffic lights	**Aux feux** o fer
At the roundabout	**Au rond-point** o ron-pwen
At the level-crossing	**Au passage à niveau** o passash ah neevo
It's near/far	**C'est près/loin** seh preh/lwen
One kilometre	**Un kilomètre** an keelomet
Two kilometres	**Deux kilomètres** der keelomet
Five minutes . . .	**Cinq minutes . . .** sank meenoot . . .
on foot	**à pied** ah pee-eh
by car	**en voiture** ahn vwah-toor
Take . . .	**Prenez . . .** prer-neh . . .
the bus	**l'autobus** lotoboos
the train	**le train** ler tran
the tram	**le tram** ler tram
the underground	**le métro** ler metro

[*For public transport, see p. 112.*]

The tourist information office

ESSENTIAL INFORMATION

- Most towns and even some villages in France have a tourist information office, run by the regional or local tourist boards.
- Look for these words:
  SYNDICAT D'INITIATIVE
  OFFICE DE TOURISME
- Sometimes there may be signposts with these abbreviations: **SI, OT** or **ESSI.**
- Information is also available from the Touring Club and Automobile Club offices, often indicated with the abbreviations **TCF** (French Touring Club) and **ACF** (French Automobile Club). **TCF** also offers a breakdown service **Touring Secours.**
- These offices give you free information in the form of printed leaflets, fold-outs, brochures, lists and plans.
- You may have to pay for some of these but this is not usual.
- For finding a tourist office, see p. 18.

WHAT TO SAY

Please, have you got ...

    a plan of the town?

    a list of hotels?

    a list of campsites?

    a list of restaurants?

    a list of coach excursions?

    a list of events?

    a leaflet on the town?

S'il vous plaît, avez-vous ...
sil voo pleh ahveh-voo ...
un plan de la ville?
an plahn der lah veel
une liste d'hôtels?
oon leest dotel
une liste de campings?
oon leest der camping
une liste de restaurants?
oon leest der restorahn
une liste d'excursions en car?
oon leest dexcoor-see-on an car
une liste d'événements?
oon leest deh-veh-ner-mahn
une brochure sur la ville?
oon broshooer soor lah veel

Please, have you got . . .	S'il vous plaît, avez-vous . . . sil voo pleh ahveh-voo . . .
a leaflet on the region?	une brochure sur la région? oon broshooer soor lah resh-yon
a railway timetable?	un horaire des trains? an orair deh tran
a bus timetable?	un horaire des autobus? an orair deh zotoboos
In English, please	En anglais, s'il vous plaît ahn ahngleh sil voo pleh
How much do I owe you?	Combien vous dois-je? combee-an voo dwahsh
Can you recommend . . .	Pouvez-vous recommander . . . pooveh-voo rer-commahndeh . . .
a cheap hotel?	un hôtel bon marché? an otel bon marsheh
a cheap restaurant?	un restaurant bon marché? an restorahn bon marsheh
Can you make a booking for me?	Pouvez-vous me faire une réservation? pooveh-voo mer fair oon rehzairvah-see-on

LIKELY ANSWERS

You need to understand when the answer is 'No'. You should be able to tell by the assistant's facial expression, tone of voice and gesture, but there are some language clues, such as:

No	Non non
I'm sorry	Je regrette sher rer-gret
I don't have a list of campsites	Je n'ai pas la liste des campings sher neh pah lah leest deh camping
I haven't got any left	Il ne m'en reste plus il ner mahn rest ploo
It's free	C'est gratuit seh grah-twee

Accommodation

Hotel

ESSENTIAL INFORMATION

- If you want hotel-type accommodation, all the following words in capital letters are worth looking for on name boards:
  HÔTEL
  MOTEL
  PENSION (a small, privately run hotel)
  AUBERGE (often picturesque type of hotel situated in the countryside)
- List of hotels and **pensions** can be obtained from local tourist offices or the Canadian Government Office of Tourism in Ottawa or the French Government Tourist Office in New York [*see p. 7*].
- The cost is displayed in the room itself, so you can check it when having a look around before agreeing to stay.
- The displayed cost is for the room itself, per night and not per person. Breakfast is extra, and therefore optional.
- Not all hotels provide meals, apart from breakfast. A **pension** always provides meals. Breakfast is continental style: coffee or tea with rolls/croissants, butter and jam.
- An identity document is requested when registering at a hotel and will normally be kept overnight. Passports or driving licences are accepted.
- Tipping: Look for the words **service compris/non compris** (service included/not included) on your bill. Tip porters.
- Finding a hotel, see p. 18.

WHAT TO SAY

I have a booking

J'ai une réservation
sheh oon rehzairvah-see-on

Have you any vacancies, please?

Avez-vous des chambres libres, s'il vous plaît?
ahveh-voo deh shahmb leeb sil voo pleh

Can I book a room?	**Puis-je réserver une chambre?**
	pweesh rehzairveh oon shahmb
It's for ...	**C'est pour ...**
	seh poor ...
one person	**une personne**
	oon pairson
two people	**deux personnes**
	der pairson

[*For numbers, see p. 126.*]

It's for ...	**C'est pour ...**
	seh poor ...
one night	**une nuit**
	oon nwee
two nights	**deux nuits**
	der nwee
one week	**une semaine**
	oon ser-men
two weeks	**deux semaines**
	der ser-men
I would like ...	**Je voudrais ...**
	sher voodreh ...
a (quiet) room	**une chambre (tranquille)**
	oon shahmb (trahnkeel)
two rooms	**deux chambres**
	der shahmb
with a single bed	**à un lit**
	ah an lee
with two single beds	**à deux lits**
	ah der lee
with a double bed	**avec un grand lit**
	ahvec an grahn lee
with a toilet	**avec WC**
	ahvec veh-seh
with a bathroom	**avec salle de bains**
	ahvec sal der ban
with a shower	**avec douche**
	ahvec doosh
with a cot	**avec un lit d'enfant**
	ahvec an lee dahnfahn
with a balcony	**avec balcon**
	ahvec bal-con

I would like ...	**Je voudrais ...**
	sher voodreh
full board	**pension complète**
	pahn-see-on complet
half board	**demi-pension**
	der-me pahn-see-on
bed and breakfast	**chambre et petit déjeuner**
	shahmb eh ptee desh-neh

[*See essential information*]

Do you serve meals?	**Est-ce que vous faites restaurant?**
	esk voo fet restorahn
At what time is ...	**A quelle heure est ...**
	ah keller eh ...
breakfast?	**le petit déjeuner?**
	ler ptee desh-neh
lunch?	**le déjeuner?**
	ler desh-neh
dinner?	**le dîner?**
	ler dee-neh
How much is it?	**C'est combien?**
	seh combee-an
Can I look at the room?	**Puis-je voir la chambre?**
	pweesh vwah lah shahmb
I'd prefer a room ...	**J'aimerais mieux une chambre ...**
	shem-reh me-er oon shahmb ...
at the front/at the back	**sur le devant/derrière**
	soor ler der-vahn/derri-air
OK, I'll take it	**D'accord, je la prends**
	daccor sher lah prahn
No thanks, I won't take it	**Non merci, je ne la prends pas**
	non mair-see sher ner lah prahn pah
The key to number (10), please	**La clé du (dix), s'il vous plaît**
	lah cleh doo (deess) sil voo pleh
Please, can I have ...	**S'il vous plaît, puis-je avoir ...**
	sil voo pleh pweesh ahvwah ...
a coat hanger?	**un cintre?**
	an sant
a towel?	**une serviette?**
	oon sairv-yet
a glass?	**un verre?**
	an vair

Please, can I have . . .	**S'il vous plaît, puis-je avoir . . .** Sil voo pleh pweesh ahvwah . . .
some soap?	**du savon?** doo sav-on
an ashtray?	**un cendrier?** an sahndree-eh
another pillow?	**un autre oreiller?** an ot oreh-yeh
another blanket?	**une autre couverture?** oon ot coovairtoor
Come in!	**Entrez!** ahntreh
One moment, please!	**Un moment, s'il vous plaît!** an mo-mahn sil voo pleh
Please can you . . .	**S'il vous plaît, pouvez-vous . . .** sil voo pleh pooveh voo . . .
do this laundry/dry-cleaning?	**laver ceci/nettoyer ceci?** lav-eh ser-see/nettwah-yeh ser-see
call me at . . . ?	**m'appeler à . . . ?** mappleh ah . . .
help me with my luggage?	**m'aider à porter mes bagages?** med-eh ah porteh meh baggash
call me a taxi for . . . ?	**m'appeler un taxi pour . . . ?** mappleh an taxee poor . . .

[*For times, see p. 128.*]

The bill, please	**La note, s'il vous plaît** lah not sil voo pleh
Is service included?	**Est-ce que le service est compris?** esk ler sairvees eh compree
I think this is wrong	**Je crois qu'il y a une erreur** sher crwah kil yah oon error
May I have a receipt?	**Puis-je avoir un reçu?** pweesh ahvwah oon rer-soo

At breakfast

Some more . . . please	**Encore . . . s'il vous plaît** ahncor . . . sil voo pleh
coffee	**du café** doo cahfeh

tea	**du thé**
	doo teh
bread	**du pain**
	doo pan
butter	**du beurre**
	doo ber
jam	**de la confiture**
	der lah confeetoor
May I have a boiled egg?	**Puis-je avoir un œuf à la coque?**
	pweesh ahvwah an erf ah lah cok

LIKELY REACTIONS

Have you an identity document, please?	**Avez-vous une pièce d'identité, s'il vous plaît?**
	ahveh-voo oon pee-ess deedahn-teeteh sil voo pleh
What's your name? [see p. 11]	**Quel est votre nom?**
	kel eh vot nom
Sorry, we're full	**Je regrette, c'est complet**
	sher rer-gret seh compleh
I haven't any rooms left	**Je n'ai plus de chambres**
	sher neh ploo der shahmb
Do you want to have a look?	**Vous voulez voir?**
	voo vooleh vwah
How many people is it for?	**C'est pour combien de personnes?**
	seh poor combee-an der pairson
From (7 o'clock) onwards	**A partir de (sept) heures**
	ah parteer der (set) er
From (midday) onwards	**A partir de (midi)**
	ah parteer der (meedee)

[For times, see p. 128.]
It's (63) francs   **C'est (soixante-trois) francs**
              seh (swah-sahnt trwah) frahn

[For numbers, see p. 126.]

Camping and youth hostelling

ESSENTIAL INFORMATION
Camping

● Look for the word **CAMPING** or this sign.

● Be prepared to have to pay:
  per person
  for the car (if applicable)
  for the tent or caravan plot
  for electricity
  for hot showers
● You must provide proof of identity such as your passport.
● You can obtain lists of campsites from local tourist offices [*see p. 18*] or from the government tourist offices [*see p. 7*].
● Some campsites offer discounts to campers with the International Camping Carnet and some offer weekly, fortnightly or monthly rates.
● Officially recognized campsites have a star rating (like hotels).
● Municipal-run campsites are often reasonably priced and well-run.
● Off-site camping (**le camping sauvage**) is prohibited in many areas. As a rule it is better and safer to use recognized sites.

Youth hostels

● Look for the words: **AUBERGE DE JEUNESSE.**
● You will be asked for a YHA card and your passport on arrival.
● Food and cooking facilities vary from hostel to hostel and you may have to help with the domestic chores.
● You must take your own sleeping bag lining but sheets can usually be hired on arrival.
● In the high season it is advisable to book beds in advance, and

your stay will be limited to a maximum of three consecutive nights
per hostel.
- Apply to the government tourist offices [*see p. 7*] or local tourist
offices in France [*see p. 18*] for lists of youth hostels and details of
regulations for hostellers.
- For buying or replacing camping equipment, see p. 52.

WHAT TO SAY

I have a booking	**J'ai une réservation** sheh oon rehzairvah-see-on
Have you any vacancies?	**Avez-vous de la place?** ahveh-voo der lah plass
It's for ...	**C'est pour ...** seh poor ...
one adult/one person	**un adulte/une personne** an ahdoolt/oon pairson
two adults/two people	**deux adultes/deux personnes** der zahdoolt/der pairson
and one child	**et un enfant** eh an ahnfahn
and two children	**et deux enfants** eh der zahnfahn
It's for ...	**C'est pour ...** seh poor ...
one night	**une nuit** oon nwee
two nights	**deux nuits** der nwee
one week	**une semaine** oon ser-men
two weeks	**deux semaines** der ser-men
How much is it ...	**C'est combien ...** seh combee-an ...
for the tent?	**pour la tente?** poor lah tahnt
for the caravan?	**pour la caravane?** poor lah caravan
for the car?	**pour la voiture?** poor lah vwah-toor

How much is it . . .	**C'est combien . . .** seh combee-an . . .
for the electricity?	**pour l'électricité?** poor leh-lectriciteh
per person?	**par personne?** par pairson
per day/night?	**par jour/nuit?** par shoor/nwee
May I look round?	**Puis-je voir?** pweesh vwah
Do you close the gate at night?	**Est-ce que vous fermez le portail la nuit?** esk-voo fairmeh ler por-ty lah nwee
Do you provide anything . . .	**Est-ce qu'on peut avoir . . .** eskon per ahvwah . . .
to eat?	**de la nourriture?** der lah nooreetoor
to drink?	**des boissons?** deh bwah-son
Is there/are there . . .	**Est-ce qu'il y a . . .** eskil yah . . .
a bar?	**un bar?** an bar
hot showers?	**des douches chaudes?** deh doosh shod
a kitchen?	**une cuisine?** oon kweezeen
a laundry?	**une laverie?** oon lav-ree
a restaurant?	**un restaurant?** an restorahn
a shop?	**un magasin?** an mahgah-**zan**
a swimming pool?	**une piscine?** oon pee-seen
a takeaway?	**des plats à emporter?** deh plah ah ahmporteh

[*For food shopping, see p. 59, and for eating and drinking out, see p. 80.*]

I would like a counter for the shower	**Je voudrais un jeton pour la douche**
	sher voodreh an sher-ton poor lah doosh
Where are …	**Où sont …**
	oo son …
the dustbins?	**les poubelles?**
	leh poobel
the showers?	**les douches?**
	leh doosh
the toilets?	**les WC?**
	leh veh-seh
At what time must one …	**A quelle heure doit-on …**
	ah keller dwah-ton …
go to bed?	**se coucher?**
	ser coosheh
get up?	**se lever?**
	ser lerveh
Please, have you got …	**S'il vous plaît, avez-vous …**
	sil voo pleh ahveh-voo …
a broom?	**un balai?**
	an bah-leh
a corkscrew?	**un tire-bouchon?**
	an teer-booshon
a drying-up cloth?	**un torchon?**
	an torshon
a fork?	**une fourchette?**
	oon foorshet
a fridge?	**un frigo?**
	an freego
a frying pan?	**une poêle?**
	oon pwahl
an iron?	**un fer à repasser?**
	an fair ah rer-passeh
a knife?	**un couteau?**
	an cooto
a plate?	**une assiette?**
	oon ass-yet
a saucepan?	**une casserole?**
	oon cass-rol
a teaspoon?	**une cuillère à café**
	oon kwee-yeh ah cahfeh

Please, have you got ...	S'il vous plait, avez-vous ... sil voo pleh ahveh-voo ...
a tin opener	un ouvre-boîte? an oov-bwaht
any washing powder?	de la lessive? der lah lesseeve
any washing-up liquid?	du liquide pour la vaisselle? doo leekeed poor lah veh-sel
The bill, please	La note, s'il vous plaît lah not sil voo pleh

Problems

The toilet	Le WC ler veh-seh
The shower	La douche lah doosh
The tap	Le robinet ler robbeeneh
The razor point	La prise pour le rasoir lah preez poor ler rah-zwah
The light	La lumiére lah loom-yair
... is not working	... ne marche pas ... ner marsh pah
My camping gas has run out	Je n'ai plus de gaz sher neh ploo der gaz

LIKELY REACTIONS

Have you an identity document?	Avez-vous une pièce d'identité? ahveh-voo oon pee-ess deedahnteeteh
Your membership card, please	Votre carte, s'il vous plaît vot cart sil voo pleh
What's your name? [see p. 14.]	Votre nom, s'il vous plaît vot nom sil voo pleh
Sorry, we're full	Je regrette, c'est complet sher rer-gret seh compleh
How many people is it for?	C'est pour combien de personnes? seh poor combee-an der pairson

How many nights is it for?	**C'est pour combien de nuits?**
	seh poor combee-an der nwee
It's (5) francs ...	**C'est (cinq) francs ...**
	seh (san) frahn ...
per day/per night	**par jour/par nuit**
	par shoor/par nwee

[*For numbers, see p. 126.*]

Rented accommodation: problem solving

ESSENTIAL INFORMATION

- If you're looking for accommodation to rent, look out for:
  A LOUER (for rent)
  APPARTEMENT (apartment)
  CHALET (part-timbered house)
  FERME (farmhouse)
  MAISON (house)
  STUDIO (small apt., studio)
  VILLA (detached house with garden)
- For arranging details of your let, see 'Hotel' p. 25.
- Key words you will meet if renting on the spot:
  les arrhes (deposit)
  lez-are
  la clé (key)
  la cleh
- Having arranged your own accommodation and arrived with the key, check the obvious basics that you take for granted at home.
  Electricity: Voltage? Razors and small appliances brought from home may need adjusting. You may need an adaptor.
  Gas: Town gas or bottled gas? Butane gas must be kept indoors, propane gas must be kept outdoors.
  Stove: Don't be surprised to find:
  the grill inside the oven, or no grill at all
  a lid covering the rings which lifts up to form a 'splash-back
  a mixture of two gas rings and two electric rings.

Toilet: Mains drainage or septic tank? Don't flush disposable diapers or anything else down the toilet if you are on a septic tank.

Water: Find the stopcock. Check taps and plugs — they may not operate in the way you are used to. Check how to turn on (or light) the hot water.

Windows: Check the method of opening and closing windows and shutters.

Insects: Is an insecticide spray provided? If not, get one locally.

Equipment: For buying or replacing equipment, see p. 52.

● You will probably have an official agent, but be clear in your own mind who to contact in an emergency, even if it is only a neighbour in the first instance.

WHAT TO SAY

My name is . . .	**Je m'appelle . . .** shmappel . . .
I'm staying at . . .	**Je suis à . . .** sher swee ah . . .
They've cut off . . .	**On a coupé . . .** on ah coopeh . . .
the electricity	**l'électricité** leh-lectricit-eh
the gas	**le gaz** ler gaz
the water	**l'eau** lo
Is there . . . in the area?	**Est-ce qu'il y a . . . par ici** eskil yah . . . par ee-see
an electrician	**un électricien** an electri-see-an
a plumber	**un plombier** an plom-bee-eh
a gas fitter	**un employé du gaz** an ahmplwah-yeh doo gaz
Where is . . .	**Où est . . .** oo eh . . .
the fuse box?	**la boîte à fusibles?** lah bwaht ah foozeeb

the stopcock?	**le robinet d'arrêt?**
	ler robbeeneh dah-reh
the boiler?	**la chaudière?**
	lah shodee-air
the water heater?	**le chauffe-eau?**
	ler shof-o
Is there ...	**Est-ce qu'il y a ...**
	eskil yah ...
town gas?	**le gaz de ville?**
	ler gaz der veel
bottled gas?	**du gaz en bouteille?**
	doo gaz ahn bootay
a septic tank?	**une fosse septique?**
	oon foss septeek
central heating?	**le chauffage central?**
	ler shofash sahntrahl
The cooker	**La cuisinière**
	lah kweezeen-yair
The hair dryer	**Le séchoir à cheveux**
	ler seh-shwah ah sher-ver
The heating	**Le chauffage**
	ler shofash
The immersion heater	**Le chauffe-bains**
	ler shof-ban
The iron	**Le fer à repasser**
	ler fair ah rer-passeh
The pilot light	**La veilleuse**
	lah veh-yerz
The refrigerator	**Le réfrigérateur**
	ler refrisheh-rahter
The telephone	**Le téléphone**
	ler telefon
The toilet	**Le WC**
	ler veh-seh
The washing machine	**La machine à laver**
	lah machine ah lahveh
... is not working	**... ne marche pas**
	... ner marsh pah
Where can I get ...	**Où puis-je trouver ...**
	oo pweesh trooveh ...
an adaptor for this?	**un adaptateur pour ceci?**
	an ah-daptahter poor ser-see

Where can I get ...	Où puis-je trouver ... oo pweesh trooveh ...
a bottle of butane gas?	une bouteille de gaz butane? oon bootay der gaz boo-tan
a bottle of propane gas?	une bouteille de gaz propane? oon bootay der gaz pro-pan
a fuse?	un fusible? an foozeeb
an insecticide spray?	une bombe insecticide? oon bomb-ansectee-seed
a light bulb?	une ampoule électrique? oon ahmpool ehlectreek
The drain	Le tuyau ler twee-yo
The sink	L'évier lev-yeh
The toilet	Le WC ler veh-seh
... is blocked	... est bouché ... eh boosheh
The gas is leaking	Il y a une fuite de gaz il ya oon fweet der gaz
Can you mend it straightaway?	Pouvez-vous le réparer tout de suite? pooveh-voo ler reh-pahreh too der sweet
When can you mend it?	Quand pouvez-vous le réparer? kahn pooveh-voo ler reh-pahreh
How much do I owe you?	Combien vous dois-je? combee-an voo dwah-sh
When is the rubbish collected?	Quand ramasse-t-on les ordures? kahn rahmass-ton leh zordoor

LIKELY REACTIONS

What's your name?	Comment vous appelez-vous? commahn voo zappleh-voo
What's your address?	Quelle est votre adresse? kel eh vot address
There's a shop ...	Il y a un magasin ... il yah an mahgahzan ...
in town/in the village	en ville/dans le village ahn veel/dahn ler veelash

I can't come ...	**Je ne peux pas venir ...**
	sher ner per pah ver-neer ...
today	**aujourd'hui**
	o-shoordwee
this week	**cette semaine**
	set ser-men
until Monday	**avant lundi**
	ahvahn lerndee
I can come ...	**Je peux venir ...**
	sher per ver-neer ...
on Tuesday	**mardi**
	mardee
when you want	**quand vous voulez**
	kahn voo vooleh
Every day	**Tous les jours**
	too leh shoor
Every other day	**Tous les deux jours**
	too leh der shoor
On Wednesdays	**Le mercredi**
	ler mairk-dee

[*For days of the week, see p. 130.*]

General shopping

The drug store/The chemist's

ESSENTIAL INFORMATION

- Look for the word
  PHARMACIE or this sign.
- Medicines (drugs) are only
  available only at a
  drug store.
- Some non-drugs can be
  bought at a supermarket
  or department store, of
  course.
- Try the drug store *before* going
  to a doctor: they are usually qualified to treat minor injuries.
- To claim money back on prescriptions, remove price labels from
  medicines, and stick them on the prescription sheet.
- Drug stores take it in turns to stay open all night and on Sundays.
  A notice on the door headed **PHARMACIE DE GARDE** or
  PHARMACIE DE SERVICE gives the address of the nearest
  pharmacist on duty.
- Some toiletries can also be bought at a **PARFUMERIE,** but they
  will probably be more expensive.
- Finding a drug store, see p. 18.

WHAT TO SAY

I'd like ...	Je voudrais ...
	sher voodreh ...
some Alka Seltzer	de l'Alka Seltzer
	der lalka seltzer
some antiseptic	un antiseptique
	an anti-septeek
some aspirin	de l'aspirine
	der laspeereen
some bandage	une bande
	oon bahnd

some cotton wool	**du coton**
	doo cotton
some eye drops	**des gouttes pour les yeux**
	deh goot poor leh zee-er
some foot powder	**une poudre anti-perspirante**
	oon pood anti-pairspeerahnt
some gauze dressing	**de la gaze**
	der lah gahz
some inhalant	**un inhalateur**
	an eenahlah-ter
some insect repellent	**une crème anti-moustiques**
	oon crem anti-moosteek
some lip salve	**de la pommade 'Rosa'**
	der lah pom-ad rozah
some nose drops	**des gouttes pour le nez**
	deh goot poor ler neh
some sticking plaster	**du sparadrap**
	doo spahrahdrah
some throat pastilles	**des pastilles pour la gorge**
	deh pass-tee poor lah gorsh
some Vaseline	**de la Vaseline**
	der lah vasleen
I'd like something for ...	**Je voudrais un produit pour ...**
	sher voodreh an prodwee poor ...
bites/stings (insect)	**les piqûres (d'insectes)**
	leh peek-oor (dan-sect)
burns/scalds	**les brûlures**
	leh brool-yoor
chilblains	**les engelures**
	leh zahn-sher-yoor
a cold	**le rhume**
	ler room
constipation	**la constipation**
	lah consteepah-see-on
a cough	**la toux**
	lah too
diarrhoea	**la diarrhée**
	lah dee-ah-reh
ear-ache	**le mal d'oreille**
	ler mal doray
flu	**la grippe**
	lah greep

I'd like something for ...	**Je voudrais un produit pour ...**
	sher voodreh an prodwee poor ...
sore gums	**la gingivite**
	lah shanshee-veet
sprains	**les entorses**
	leh zahntorss
sunburn	**les coups de soleil**
	leh coo der solay
travel sickness	**le mal de mer**
	ler mal der mair
I'd like ...	**Je voudrais ...**
	sher voodreh ...
some baby food	**de la nourriture pour bébés**
	der lah nooreetoor poor behbeh
some contraceptives	**des contraceptifs**
	deh contraceptif
some deodorant	**un déodorant**
	an deh-odorahn
some disposable nappies	**des couches en cellulose**
	deh coosh ahn celluloz
some handcream	**de la crème pour les mains**
	der lah crem poor leh man
some lipstick	**du rouge à lèvres**
	doo roosh ah lev
some make-up remover	**un démaquillant**
	an dehmahkee-yahn
some paper tissues	**des Kleenex**
	deh kleenex
some razor blades	**des lames de rasoir**
	deh lam der rahzwah
some safety pins	**des épingles de sûreté**
	dez ehpang der soor-teh
some sanitary towels	**des serviettes périodiques**
	deh sairv-yet pehree-odeek
some shaving cream	**de la crème à raser**
	der lah crem ah rahzeh
some soap	**du savon**
	doo sav-on
some suntan lotion/oil	**une crème/huile solaire**
	oon crem/weel solair

some talcum powder	**du talc**
	doo talc
some Tampax	**des Tampax**
	deh tampax
some toilet paper	**du papier hygiénique**
	doo pap-yeh eeshee-ehneek
some toothpaste	**du dentifrice**
	doo dahnteefreess

[*For other essential expressions, see 'Shop Talk', p. 54.*]

Holiday items

ESSENTIAL INFORMATION

- Places to shop at and signs to look for:
  LIBRAIRIE-PAPÈTERIE (stationery/book store)
  BUREAU DE TABAC (smoke shop)
  CARTES POSTALES — SOUVENIRS (postcards — souvenirs)
  PHOTOGRAPHIE (films and photographic equipment)
- and the main department stores:
  MONOPRIX
  PRISUNIC
  INNO

WHAT TO SAY

Where can I buy . . . ?	**Où puis-je acheter . . . ?**
	oo pweesh ashteh . . .
I'd like . . .	**Je voudrais . . .**
	sher voodreh . . .
a bag	**un sac**
	an sac
a beach ball	**un ballon pour la plage**
	an bah-lon poor lah plash
a bucket	**un seau**
	an so
an English newspaper	**un journal anglais**
	an shoornahl ahngleh
some envelopes	**des enveloppes**
	deh zahnv-lop
a guide book	**un guide**
	an gheed
a map (of the area)	**une carte (de la région)**
	oon cart (der lah resh-yon)
some postcards	**des cartes postales**
	deh cart postahl
a spade	**une pelle**
	oon pel
a straw hat	**un chapeau de paille**
	an shahpo der pie

a suitcase	**une valise**
	oon val-eez
some sunglasses	**des lunettes de soleil**
	deh loonet der solay
a sunshade	**un parasol**
	an parasol
an umbrella	**un parapluie**
	an para-plwee
some writing paper	**du papier à lettres**
	doo pap-yeh ah let
I'd like ... [show the camera]	**Je voudrais ...**
	sher voodreh ...
a colour film	**un rouleau de pellicules couleur**
	an roolo der pelleecool cooler
a black and white film	**un rouleau de pellicules noir et blanc**
	an roolo der pelleecool nwah eh blahn
for prints	**pour photos**
	poor photo
for slides	**pour diapositives**
	poor dee-ah-positive
12 (24/36) exposures	**douze (vingt-quatre/trente-six) poses**
	dooz (vant-cat/trahnt-see) pose
a standard 8 mm film	**un film ordinaire huit millimètres**
	an film ordeenair wee meeleemet
a super 8 film	**un film super huit**
	an film soopair weet
some flash bulbs	**des flash**
	deh flash
This camera is broken	**Cet appareil ne marche plus**
	set appahray ner marsh ploo
The film is stuck	**Le film est coincé**
	ler film eh kwen-seh
Please can you ...	**S'il vous plaît, pouvez-vous ...**
	sil voo pleh pooveh-voo ...
develop/print this?	**développer/tirer ceci?**
	dev-loppeh/tee-reh ser-see
load the camera for me?	**charger l'appareil?**
	shar-sheh lappahray

[For other essential expressions, see 'Shop talk', p. 54.]

The smoke shop

ESSENTIAL INFORMATION

- Tobacco is sold only where you see these signs.
- A smoke shop is called a **BUREAU DE TABAC**.
- See p. 18 to ask if there is one nearby.
- Smoke shops always sell postage stamps.
- A smoke shop is sometimes part of a café (**CAFÉ-TABAC**), a stationery store (**PAPÈTERIE**) or newsstand (**TABAC-JOURNAUX**).

WHAT TO SAY

A packet of cigarettes ...	**Un paquet de cigarettes ...**
	an pak-eh der cigarette ...
with filters	**à bout filtre**
	ah boo feelt
without filters	**sans filtre**
	sahn feelt
king size	**longues**
	long
menthol	**à la menthe**
	ah lah mahnt
Those up there ...	**Celles-là, en haut ...**
	cell-lah ahn o ...
on the right	**à droite**
	ah drwaht
on the left	**à gauche**
	ah goshe

These [*point*]	**Celles-ci**
	cell-see
Cigarettes, please	**Des cigarettes, s'il vous plaît . . .**
	deh cigarette, sil voo pleh . . .
100, 200, 300	**cent, deux cents, trois cents**
	sahn, der sahn, trwah sahn
Two packets	**Deux paquets**
	der pak-eh
Have you got . . .	**Avez-vous . . .**
	ahveh-voo . . .
English cigarettes?	**des cigarettes anglaises?**
	deh cigarette ahnglez
American cigarettes?	**des cigarettes américaines?**
	deh cigarette ameriken
English pipe tobacco?	**du tabac de pipe anglais?**
	doo tahbah der peep ahngleh
American pipe tobacco?	**du tabac de pipe américain?**
	doo tahbah der peep american
rolling tobacco?	**du tabac à rouler?**
	doo tahbah ah rooleh
A packet of pipe tobacco	**Un paquet de tabac de pipe**
	an pak-eh der tahbah der peep
That one down there . . .	**Celui-là, en bas . .**
	ser-lwee-lah ahn bah . . .
on the right	**à droite**
	ah drwaht
on the left	**à gauche**
	ah goshe
This one [*point*]	**Celui-ci**
	ser-lwee-see
A cigar, please	**Un cigare, s'il vous plaît**
	an cigar sil voo pleh
That one [*point*]	**Celui-là**
	ser-lwee-lah
Some cigars	**Des cigares**
	deh cigar
Those [*point*]	**Ceux-là**
	ser-lah
A box of matches	**Une boîte d'allumettes**
	oon bwaht dalloomet
A packet of pipe-cleaners	**Un paquet de cure-pipes**
	an pak-eh der cooer peep

A packet of flints	**Un paquet de pierres**
[show lighter]	an pak-eh der pee-air
Lighter fuel	**De l'essence à briquet**
	der lessahns ah breekeh
Lighter gas, please	**Du gaz pour briquet, s'il vous plaît**
	doo gaz poor breekeh sil voo pleh

[*For other essential expressions, see 'Shop Talk', p. 54.*]

Buying clothes

ESSENTIAL INFORMATION

- Look for:
  CONFECTION DAMES (women's clothes)
  CONFECTION HOMMES (men's clothes)
  CHAUSSURES (shoes)
- Don't buy without being measured first or without trying things on.
- Don't rely on coversion charts of clothing sizes [*see p. 141*].
- If you are buying for someone else, take their measurements with you (in centimetres).
- The department stores **MONOPRIX** and **PRISUNIC** sell clothes and shoes.

WHAT TO SAY

I'd like ...	**Je voudrais ...**
	sher voodreh ...
an anorak	**un anorak**
	an anorak
a belt	**une ceinture**
	oon centoor
a bikini	**un bikini**
	an bikini

a blouse	**un chemisier**
	an sher-meez-yeh
a bra	**un soutien-gorge**
	an soot-yen-gorsh
some briefs (women)	**une culotte**
	oon coolot
a cap (swimming/skiing)	**un bonnet (de bain/de ski)**
	an bonneh (der ban/der skee)
a cardigan	**un cardigan**
	an cardeegahn
a coat	**un manteau**
	an mahnto
a dress	**une robe**
	oon rob
a hat	**un chapeau**
	an shahpo
a jacket	**une veste**
	oon vest
some jeans	**un jean**
	an jean
a jumper/pullover	**un pullover**
	an poolovair
a nightdress	**une chemise de nuit**
	oon sher-meez der nwee
some pyjamas	**un pyjama**
	an peeshah-mah
a raincoat	**un imperméable**
	an ampair-meh-ab
a shirt (man's)	**une chemise**
	oon sher-meez
some shorts	**un short**
	an short
a skirt	**une jupe**
	oon shoop
a suit (man's)	**un costume**
	an costoom
a suit (woman's)	**un ensemble**
	an ahn-sahmb
a swimsuit	**un maillot de bain**
	an mah-yo der ban
some tights	**un collant**
	an collahn

I'd like ...	**Je voudrais ...**
	sher voodreh
some trousers	**un pantalon**
	an pahntah-lon
a T-shirt	**un tee-shirt**
	an tee-shirt
some underpants (men)	**un slip**
	an sleep
I'd like a pair of ...	**Je voudrais une paire de ...**
	sher voodreh oon pair der ...
gloves	**gants**
	gahn
socks	**chaussettes**
	sho-set
stockings	**bas**
	bah
I'd like a pair of ...	**Je voudrais une paire de ...**
	sher voodreh oon pair der ...
shoes	**chaussures**
	sho-sooer
canvas shoes	**chaussures en toile**
	sho-sooer ahn twahl
sandals	**sandales**
	sahndahl
beach shoes	**nu-pieds**
	noo pee-eh
smart shoes	**chaussures habillées**
	sho-sooer ahbee-yeh
boots	**bottes**
	bot
mocassins	**mocassins**
	mo-cah-san
My size is ...	**Je prends du ...**
[*For numbers, see p. 126*]	sher prahn doo ...
Can you measure me, please?	**Pouvez-vous me mesurer, s'il vous plaît?**
	pooveh-voo mer mer-zoo-reh sil voo pleh
Can I try it on?	**Puis-je l'essayer?**
	pweesh lesseh-yeh
It's for a present	**C'est pour un cadeau**
	seh poor an cahdo

These are the measurements	**Voici les mesures**
[*Show written*]	vwah-see leh mer-zooer
bust/chest	**poitrine**
	pwahtreen
collar	**tour de cou**
	toor der coo
hips	**hanches**
	ahnsh
leg	**jambe**
	shahmb
shoulders	**épaules**
	ehpol
waist	**taille**
	tie
Have you got something . . .	**Avez-vous quelque chose . . .**
	ahveh-voo kelk shoz . . .
in black?	**en noir?**
	ahn nwah
in white?	**en blanc?**
	ahn blahn
in grey?	**en gris?**
	ahn gree
in blue?	**en bleu?**
	ahn bler
in brown?	**en marron?**
	ahn mah-ron
in pink?	**en rose?**
	ahn rose
in green	**en vert?**
	ahn vair
in red?	**en rouge?**
	ahn roosh
in yellow?	**en jaune?**
	ahn shon
in this colour [*point*]	**de cette couleur?**
	der set cooler
in cotton?	**en coton?**
	ahn cot-on
in denim?	**en toile?**
	ahn twahl
in leather?	**en cuir?**
	ahn kweer

Have you got something ...	Avez-vous quelque chose ...
	ahveh-voo kelk shoz ...
in nylon?	en nylon?
	ahn neelon
in suede?	en daim?
	ahn dan
in wool?	en laine?
	ahn len
in this material? [point]	dans ce tissu?
	dahn ser tee-soo

[For other essential expressions, see 'Shop talk', p. 54.]

Replacing equipment

ESSENTIAL INFORMATION

● Look out for these shops and signs:
  QUINCAILLERIE (hardware)
  ÉLECTRO-MÉNAGER (electrical goods)
  DROGUERIE (household cleaning materials)
● In a supermarket, look for this display: **ENTRETIEN**
● To ask the way to the shop, see p. 18.
● At a campsite try their shop first.

WHAT TO SAY

Have you got ...	Avez-vous ...
	ahveh-voo ...
an adaptor? [show appliance]	un adaptateur?
	an ahdap-tahter
a bottle of butane gas?	une bouteille de gaz butane?
	oon bootay der gaz boo-tan
a bottle of propane gas?	une bouteille de propane?
	oon bootay der pro-pan
a bottle opener?	un ouvre-bouteille?
	an oov-bootay

a corkscrew?	un tire-bouchon? an teer-booshon
any disinfectant?	un désinfectant? an deh-zanfectahn
any disposable cups?	des gobelets à jeter? deh gob-leh ah sheteh
any disposable plates?	des assiettes à jeter? dez ass-yet ah sheteh
a drying-up cloth?	un torchon? an torshon
any forks?	des fourchettes? deh foorshet
a fuse? [*show old one*]	un fusible? an foozeeb
an insecticide spray?	une bombe insecticide? oon bomb-ansectee-seed
a paper kitchen roll?	du sopalin? doo sopahlan
any knives?	des couteaux? deh cooto
a light bulb? [*show old one*]	une ampoule? oon ahmpool
a plastic bucket?	un seau en plastique? an so ahn plasteek
a scouring pad?	un tampon pour récurer? an tahmpon poor reh-cooreh
a spanner?	une clé plate? oon cleh plat
a sponge?	une éponge? oon ehponsh
any string?	de la ficelle? der lah feecell
any tent pegs?	des piquets de tente? deh peekeh der tahnt
a tin opener?	un ouvre-boîte? an oov-bwaht
a torch?	une lampe de poche? oon lahmp der posh
any torch batteries?	des piles pour lampe électrique? deh peel poor lahmp electreek
a universal plug (for the sink)?	un tampon universel (pour évier)? an tahmpon ooneevair-sel (poor ev-yeh)

Have you got ...	Avez-vous ...
	ahveh-voo ...
a washing line?	une corde à linge?
	oon cord ah lansh
any washing powder?	de la lessive?
	der lah lesseeve
any washing-up liquid?	du liquide pour la vaisselle?
	doo leekeed poor lah veh-sell
a washing-up brush?	une brosse pour la vaisselle?
	oon bross poor lah veh-sell

[*For other essential expressions, see 'Shop talk', below.*]

Shop talk

ESSENTIAL INFORMATION

- Know your coins and bills: see illustration.
  bills: 10F, 50F, 100F, 500F
  [*for numbers, see p. 126.*]
- Know how to say the important weights and measures:

50 grams	**cinquante grammes**
	sankahnt gram
100 grams	**cent grammes**
	sahn gram
200 grams	**deux cents grammes**
	der sahn gram
½ kilo	**un demi-kilo**
	an der-me keelo
1 kilo	**un kilo**
	an keelo
2 kilos	**deux kilos**
	der keelo
½ litre	**un demi-litre**
	an der-me leet
1 litre	**un litre**
	an leet
2 litres	**deux litres**
	der leet

● In small shops don't be surprised if customers, as well as the shop
assistant, say 'hello' and 'goodbye' to you.

CUSTOMER

Hello Good morning]	**Bonjour** bonshoor
Goodbye	**Au revoir** o-revwah
I'm just looking	**Je regarde** sher rer-gard
Excuse me	**Pardon** par-don
How much is this/that?	**C'est combien ça?** seh combee-an sah
What is that/what are those?	**Qu'est-ce que c'est ça?** kesk seh sah
Is there a discount?	**Est-ce que vous faites une remise?** esk voo fet oon rer-meez
I'd like that, please	**Je voudrais ça, s'il vous plaît** sher voodreh sah sil voo pleh
Not that	**Pas ça** pah sah
Like that	**Comme ça** com sah
That's enough, thank you	**Ça suffit, merci** sah soofee mair-see
More please	**Encore un peu, s'il vous plaît** ahncor an per sil voo pleh
Less please	**Moins, s'il vous plaît** mwen sil voo pleh
That's fine] OK	**Ça va** sah vah
I won't take it, thank you	**Merci je ne le prends pas** mair-see sher ner ler prahn pah
It's not right	**Ça ne va pas** sah ner vah pah
Thank you very much	**Merci bien** mair-see bee-an

Have you got something . . .	**Avez-vous quelque chose . . .** ahveh-voo kelk shoz . . .
better?	**de mieux?** dee me-er
cheaper?	**de moins cher?** der mwen shair
different?	**de différent?** der dee-fay-rahn
larger?	**de plus grand?** der ploo grahn
smaller?	**de plus petit?** der ploo ptee
At what time do you . . .	**A quelle heure . . .** ah keller . . .
open?	**ouvrez-vous?** oovreh-voo
close?	**fermez-vous?** fairmeh-voo
Can I have a bag, please?	**Puis-je avoir un sac, s'il vous plaît?** Pweesh ahvwah an sac sil voo pleh
Can I have a receipt?	**Puis-je avoir un reçu?** pweesh ahvwah an rer-soo
Do you take . . .	**Acceptez-vous . . .** accepteh-voo . . .
English/American money?	**l'argent anglais/américain?** larshahn ahngleh/american
travellers' cheques?	**les traveller chèques?** leh traveller sheck
credit cards?	**la carte bleue?** lah cart bler
I'd like . . .	**J'en voudrais . . .** shahn voodreh . . .
one like that	**un comme ça** an com sah
two like that	**deux comme ça** der com sah

SHOP ASSISTANT

Can I help you?	**Qu'y a-t-il pour votre service?** kee ah-til poor vot sairvees
What would you like?	**Vous désirez?** voo dehzeereh
Will that be all?	**Ce sera tout?** ser ser-rah too
Is that all?	**C'est tout?** seh too
Anything else?	**Vous désirez autre chose?** voo dehzeereh ot shoz
Would you like it wrapped?	**Je vous l'enveloppe?** sher voo lahnv-lop
Sorry, none left	**Je regrette, il n'y en a plus** sher rer-gret il nee ahn-nah ploo
I haven't got any	**Je n'en ai pas** sher nahn-neh pah
I haven't got any more	**Je n'en ai plus** sher nahn-neh ploo
How many do you want? How much do you want?]	**Vous en voulez combien?** voo-zahn vooleh combee-an
Is that enough?	**Ça suffit?** sah soofee

Shopping for food

Bread

ESSENTIAL INFORMATION

- Finding a bakers, see p. 19.
- Key words to look for:
  BOULANGERIE   (baker's)
  BOULANGER   (baker)
  PAIN   (bread)
- Hypermarkets, supermarkets of any size and general stores nearly always sell bread.
- Small bakers are usually open between 7.30 a.m. and 7/8 p.m. Most close on Mondays and public holidays but open on Sunday mornings.
- The most characteristic kind of loaf is the 'French stick', which comes in a number of sizes.
- For any other type of loaf, say **'un pain'** (an pan) and point.

WHAT TO SAY

Some bread, please	**Du pain, s'il vous plaît** doo pan sil voo pleh
A loaf (like that)	**Un pain (comme ça)** an pan (com sah)
A French stick	**Une baguette** oon bah-get
A large one	**Une grande** oon grahnd
A long, thin one	**Une ficelle** oon feesel
Half a French stick	**Une demi-baguette** oon der-me bah-get
A brown loaf	**Un pain intégral** an pan an-tay-gral
A bread roll	**Un petit pain** an ptee pan

A crescent roll	**Un croissant**
	an crwah-sahn
A small milk loaf bun	**Une brioche**
	oon bree-osh
A small sweet bun with sultanas	**Un pain aux raisins**
	an pan o rehzan
A small bun of brioche texture with dark chocolate filling	**Un pain au chocolat**
	an pan o shocolah
Two loaves	**Deux pains**
	der pan
Two French sticks	**Deux baguettes**
	der bah-get
Four bread rolls	**Quatre petits pains**
	kat ptee pan
Four crescent rolls	**Quatre croissants**
	kat crwah-sahn

[*For other essential expressions, see 'Shop talk', p. 54.*]

Cakes

ESSENTIAL INFORMATION

- Key words to look for:
  PÂTISSERIE (cake shop)
  PÂTISSIER (cake/pastry maker)
  PÂTISSERIES (pastries/cakes)
- To find a cake shop, see p. 18.
- **SALON DE THÉ**: a room, usually off a pâtisserie, where customers sit at tables and are served with cakes, ices, soft drinks, tea, coffee or chocolate. See p. 80, 'Ordering a drink'.
- Pâtisseries are open on Sundays, but not on Mondays.

WHAT TO SAY

The types of cakes you find in the shops vary from region to region, but the following are some of the most common.

un éclair an eclair	an eclair
un chou à la crème an shoo ah lah crem	choux pastry filled with vanilla cream
une religieuse oon rer-leeshee-erz	choux pastry in the shape of a small cottage loaf with coffee cream filling (literally: a nun)
un baba au rhum an bahbah o rom	a rum baba
un millefeuille an meelfey	alternate layers of puff pastry and almond cream
un chausson aux pommes an sho-son o pom	an apple turnover
un pet de nonne an peh der non	a doughnut
une tartelette aux pommes oon tartlet o pom	a small apple tart
. . . aux fraises . . . o frez	. . . strawberry
. . . aux abricots . . . o-zahbreeco	. . . apricot

You usually buy medium-size cakes by number:

Two doughnuts, please

Deux pets de nonne, s'il vous plaît
der peh der non, sil voo pleh

Half a dozen cream cakes

**Une demi-douzaine de gâteaux à
la crème**
oon der-me doozen der gahto ah
lah crem

You buy small cakes by weight:

200 grams of petits fours

Deux cents grammes de petits fours
der sahn gram der ptee foor

400 grams of biscuits

Quatre cents grammes de biscuits
kat sahn gram der bee-skwee

You may want to buy a larger cake by the slice:

One slice of apple cake

Une tranche de gâteau aux pommes
oon trahnsh der gahto o pom

Two slices of almond cake

Deux tranches de gâteau aux amandes
der trahnsh der gahto o-zahmahnd

You may also want to say:

A selection, please

Mélangés, s'il vous plaît
mel-ahnsheh sil voo pleh

[*For other essential expressions, see 'Shop talk', p. 54.*]

Ice-cream and sweets

ESSENTIAL INFORMATION

- Key words to look for:
  GLACES (ice-creams)
  GLACIER (ice-cream maker/seller)
  CONFISERIE (sweet shop)
  CONFISEUR (sweet maker/seller)
  PÂTISSIER (cake/pastry maker)
- Best known ice-cream brand names are:
  FRIGÉCRÈME **MOTTA**
  GERVAIS **SKI**
  MIKO
- Prepacked sweets are available in general stores and supermarkets.

WHAT TO SAY

A ... ice, please	**Une glace ... s'il vous plaît**
	oon glass ... sil voo pleh
banana	**à la banane**
	ah lah bah-nan
chocolate	**au chocolat**
	o shocolah
coffee	**au moka**
	o mokah
pistachio	**à la pistache**
	ah lah pee-stash
raspberry	**à la framboise**
	ah lah frahm-bwahz
strawberry	**à la fraise**
	ah lah frez
vanilla	**à la vanille**
	ah lah vahneel
Two francs worth	**Deux francs**
	der frahn
A single cone [*specify flavour, as above*]	**Un cornet simple**
	an corneh samp

Two single cones	**Deux cornets simples**
	der corneh samp
A double cone	**Un cornet double**
	an corneh doob
Two double cones	**Deux cornets doubles**
	der corneh doob
A mixed cone [*specify flavours, as above*]	**Un cornet mélangé**
	an corneh mel-ahnsheh
A tub	**Un carton**
	an carton
A lollipop	**Une sucette**
	oon soo-set
A packet of ...	**Un paquet de ...**
	an pak-eh der ...
100 grams of ...	**Cent grammes de ...**
	sahn gram der ...
200 grams of ...	**Deux cents grammes de ...**
	der sahn gram der ...
sweets	**bonbons**
	bonbon
toffees	**caramels**
	caramel
chocolates	**chocolats**
	shocolah
mints	**bonbons à la menthe**
	bonbon ah lah mahnt

[*For other essential expressions, see 'Shop talk', p. 54.*]

In the supermarket

ESSENTIAL INFORMATION

- The place to ask for: [*see p. 18*]
UN SUPERMARCHÉ	(supermarket)
UN HYPERMARCHÉ	(hypermarket)
UNE SUPERETTE	(corner self-service)
UNE ALIMENTATION GÉNÉRALE	(general food store)
- Key instructions on signs in the shop:
ENTRÉE	(entrance)
ENTRÉE INTERDITE	(no entry)
SORTIE	(exit)
SORTIE INTERDITE	(no exit)
SANS ISSUE	(no way out)
SORTIE SANS ACHATS	(exit for non-buyers)
CAISSE	(check-out, cash desk)
CAISSE RAPIDE	(check-out for 6 items or less)
EN RÉCLAME	(on offer)
LIBRE SERVICE	(self-service)
CHARIOTS	(trolleys)
- Opening times vary but most shops are open between 8 a.m. and 7 p.m. Hypermarkets will often remain open until 10 p.m. Remember, however, that the majority of shops are closed on Mondays.
- No need to say anything in a supermarket, but ask if you can't see what you want.
- For non-food items, see 'Replacing equipment', p. 48.

WHAT TO SAY

Excuse me, please	**Pardonnez-moi, s'il vous plaît**
	par-don-neh mwah sil voo pleh
Where is ...	**Où est ...**
	oo eh ...
the bread?	**le pain?**
	ler pan
the butter?	**le beurre?**
	ler ber

Where is . . .	Où est . . .
	oo eh . . .
the cheese?	le fromage?
	ler fromash
the chocolate?	le chocolat?
	ler shocolah
the coffee?	le café?
	ler cahfeh
the cooking oil?	l'huile?
	lweel
the fish (fresh)?	le poisson?
	ler pwah-son
the jam?	la confiture?
	lah confeetoor
the meat?	la viande?
	la vee-ahnd
the milk?	le lait?
	ler leh
the mineral water?	l'eau minérale?
	lo mee-nehrahl
the salt?	le sel?
	ler sel
the sugar?	le sucre?
	ler sook
the tea?	le thé?
	ler teh
the tinned fish?	le poisson en conserve?
	ler pwah-son ahn con-sairv
the vinegar?	le vinaigre?
	ler vee-neg
the wine?	le vin?
	ler van
Where are . . .	Où sont . . .
	oo son . . .
the biscuits?	les biscuits?
	leh biskwee
the crisps?	les pommes chips?
	leh pom ship
the eggs?	les œufs?
	leh zer
the frozen foods?	les produits surgelés?
	leh prodwee soorsh-leh

the fruit juices?	les jus de fruits?
	leh shoo der frwee
the pastas?	les pâtes?
	leh pat
the seafoods?	les fruits de mer?
	leh frwee der mair
the snails?	les escargots?
	leh zescargo
the soft drinks?	les boissons?
	leh bwah-son
the sweets?	les bonbons?
	leh bonbon
the tinned vegetables?	les légumes en conserve?
	leh lehgoom ahn con-sairv
the vegetables?	les légumes?
	leh lehgoom
Where is . . .	Où sont . . .
	oo son . . .
the fruit?	les fruits?
	leh frwee
the tinned fruit?	les fruits en conserve?
	leh frwee ahn con-sairv
the yogurt?	les yaourts?
	leh yah-oor

[For other essential expressions, see 'Shop talk', p. 54.]

Picnic food

ESSENTIAL INFORMATION

- Key words to look for:
  CHARCUTERIE   (pork butcher's, delicatessen)
  TRAITEUR   (delicatessen)
  CHARCUTIER   (pork butcher)
- In these shops you can buy a wide variety of food such as ham, salami, cheese, olives, appetizers, sausages and freshly made takeaway dishes. Specialities differ from region to region.
- Weight guide:
  4–6 oz/150 g of prepared salad per two people, if eaten as a starter to a substantial meal.
  3–4 oz/100 g of prepared salad per person, if eaten at the main part of a picnic-type meal.

WHAT TO SAY

A slice of ...	Une tranche de ...
	oon trahnsh der ...
Two slices of ...	Deux tranches de ...
	der trahnsh der ...
garlic sausage	saucisson à l'ail
	so-see-son ah lie
ham (cooked)	jambon cuit
	shahmbon kwee
ham (cured)	jambon cru
	shahmbon croo
pâté	pâté
	pahteh
roast beef	rôti de bœuf
	rotee der berf
roast pork	rôti de porc
	rotee der por
salami	saucisson
	so-see-son
100 grams of ...	Cent grammes de* ...
	sahn gram der ...

150 grams of ...	**Cent cinquante grammes de* ...**
	sahn sankahnt gram der ...
200 grams of ...	**Deux cents grammes de* ...**
	der sahn gram der ...
300 grams of ...	**Trois cents grammes de* ...**
	trwah sahn gram der ...
Russian salad	**salade russe**
	sal-ad rooss
tomato salad	**salade de tomates**
	sal-ad der tomaht
olives	**olives**
	oleev
anchovies	**anchois**
	ahn-shwah
cheese	**fromage**
	fromash

* Use d' in front of words beginning with a vowel.

You might also like to try some of these:

andouille	tripe sausage
ahn-dooy	
barquette de crevettes	boat-shaped pastry case with prawn
barket der crer-vet	filling
bœuf aux champignons	diced beef cooked with wine and
berf o shahmpeen-yon	mushrooms
... aux olives	sliced beef cooked with wine and
... o zoleev	olives
... en daube	diced beef in a thick wine sauce
... ahn dobe	
bouchée à la reine	vol-au-vent case filled with sweet-
boo-shay ah lah rain	breads and mushrooms in cream
	sauce
boudin	black pudding
boo-dain	
brandade de morue	salt cod, crushed and mixed with
brahn-dad der moroo	oil, cream and garlic
champignons à la grecque	mushrooms cooked in wine,
shahmpeen-yon ah lah grec	tomatoes and spices
cœurs d'artichaux	artichoke hearts
ker dar-tee-sho	

macédoine de légumes masshe-dwan der lehgoom	diced vegetables in mayonnaise
œufs mayonnaise er my-onez	hard boiled eggs with mayonnaise
quiche lorraine keesh lorren	egg and ham/bacon pie
rillettes ree-yet	minced pork (goose or duck) baked in fat
rouleau au fromage roolo o fromash	pastry roll with creamy cheese filling
salade niçoise sal-ad nee-swahz	tomato, potato, egg, anchovy, tunny fish and olive salad in oil and vinegar
saucisse de Strasbourg so-seess der strasboor	frankfurter
saucisson sec so-see-son sec	smoked garlic sausage
tarte à l'oignon tart ah lonion	onion pie
tarte au fromage tart o fromash	cheese pie
tomates farcies tomaht far-see	stuffed tomatoes
Brie bree	creamy white cheese
Camembert cahmahmbair	full fat soft white cheese
Emmental emmentahl	Swiss cheese with big holes
fromage de chèvre fromash der shev	goat's cheese
Gruyère gru-yair	Swiss cheese, rich in flavour, smooth in texture
Pont l'Évêque pon leh-vek	soft, runny cheese with holes, strong flavour
Roquefort rockfor	resembles Stilton

[*For other essential expressions, see 'Shop talk', p. 54.*]

Fruit and vegetables

ESSENTIAL INFORMATION

● Key words to look for:
FRUITS	(fruit)
LÉGUMES	(vegetables)
PRIMEURS	(fresh fruit and vegetables)
FRUITIER	(fruit seller)
MARCHÉ	(market)

● If possible, buy fruit and vegetables in the market where they are cheaper and fresher than in the shops. Open-air markets are held once or twice a week in most areas (or daily in large towns), usually in the mornings.
● It is customary for you to choose your own fruit and vegetables at the market (and in some shops) and for the stallholder to weigh and price them. You must take your own shopping bag: paper and plastic bags are not normally provided.
● Weight guide: 1 kg of potatoes is sufficient for six people for one meal.

WHAT TO SAY

½ kilo (1 lb) of ...
Un demi-kilo de* ...
an der-me keelo der ...

1 kilo of ...
Un kilo de* ...
an keelo der ...

2 kilos of ...
Deux kilos de* ...
der keelo der ...

  apples
  pommes
  pom

  bananas
  bananes
  bah-nan

  cherries
  cerises
  ser-eez

  grapes (white/black)
  raisins (blancs/noirs)
  rehzan (blahn/nwah)

  oranges
  oranges
  orahnsh

2 kilos of ...	**Deux kilos de* ...**
	der keelo der ...
peaches	**pêches**
	pesh
pears	**poires**
	pwah
plums	**prunes**
	proon
strawberries	**fraises**
	frez
A grapefruit, please	**Un pamplemousse, s'il vous plaît**
	an pahmp-mousse sil voo pleh
A melon	**Un melon**
	an mer-lon
A pineapple	**Un ananas**
	an ahnahnah
A water melon	**Une pastèque**
	oon passtek
250 grams of ...	**Deux cents cinquante grammes de* ...**
	der sahn sankahnt gram der ...
½ kilo of ...	**Un demi-kilo de* ...**
	an der-me keelo der ...
1 kilo of ...	**Un kilo de* ...**
	an keelo der ...
1½ kilos of ...	**Un kilo et demi de* ...**
	an keelo eh der-me der ...
2 kilos of ...	**Deux kilos de* ...**
	der keelo der ...
asparagus	**asperges**
	aspersh
carrots	**carottes**
	car-rot
green beans	**haricots verts**
	ahreeco vair
leeks	**poireaux**
	pwah-ro
mushrooms	**champignons**
	shahmpeen-yon
onions	**oignons**
	onion
peas	**petits pois**
	ptee pwah

* Use **d'** in front of words beginning with a vowel.

peppers (green/red)	**poivrons (verts/rouges)**
	pwah-vron (vair/roosh)
potatoes	**pommes de terre**
	pom der tair
shallots	**échalotes**
	eh-shallot
spinach	**épinards**
	ehpeenar
tomatoes	**tomates**
	tomaht
A bunch of parsley	**Un bouquet de persil**
	an bookeh der pair-see
A bunch of radishes	**Une botte de radis**
	oon bot der rahdee
A head of garlic	**Une tête d'ail**
	oon tet die
A lettuce	**Une salade**
	oon sal-ad
A cauliflower	**Un chou-fleur**
	an shoo-fler
A cabbage	**Un chou**
	an shoo
A stick of celery	**Un pied de céleri**
	an pee-eh der seleree
A cucumber	**Un concombre**
	an concomb
Like that, please	**Comme ça, s'il vous plaît**
	com sah sil voo pleh

These are some vegetables which may not be familiar:

aubergines obairsheen	egg-plants – purple and shiny
blettes blet	sea-kale
courgettes coorshet	very small marrows
fenouil fer-nooy	fennels – crunchy vegetables with aniseed flavour

[For other essential expressions, see 'Shop talk', p. 54.]

Meat

ESSENTIAL INFORMATION

- Key words to look for:
  BOUCHERIE   (butcher's)
  BOUCHER   (butcher)
- Weight guide: 4–6 oz/125–200 g of meat per person for one meal.
- The diagrams opposite are to help you make sense of labels on counters and supermarket displays, and decide which cut or joint to have. Translations do not help, and you don't need to say the French word involved.

WHAT TO SAY

For a joint, choose the type of meat and then say how many people it is for:

Some beef, please	**Du bœuf, s'il vous plaît** doo berf sil voo pleh
Some lamb	**De l'agneau** der lan-yo
Some mutton	**Du mouton** doo mooton
Some pork	**Du porc** doo por
Some veal	**Du veau** doo vo
A joint ...	**Un rôti ...** an rotee ...
for two people	**pour deux personnes** poor der pair-son
for four people	**pour quatre personnes** poor kat pair-son
for six people	**pour six personnes** poor see pair-son

Beef Bœuf

1 Aiguillette baronne
2 Romsteck
3 Tranche grasse
4 Gîte à la noix
5 Gîte-gîte
6 Bavette (pot-au-feu)
7 Contre-filet
8 Entrecôtes
9 Paleron
10 Flanchet
11 Tendron
12 Plat de côtes
13 Second talon
14 Veine grasse
15 Macreuse
16 Poitrine
17 Gîte-gîte

Veal Veau

1 Côtes découvertes
2 Collier
3 Epaule
4 Jarret de devant
5 Côtes secondes
6 Côtes premières
7 Flanchet
8 Longe
9 Quasi
10 Sous-noix
11 Noix pâtissière
12 Jarret

Pork Porc

1 Filet
2 Pointe
3 Jambon
4 Ventre
5 Côtes premières
6 Côtes découvertes
7 Echine
8 Tête
9 Epaule
10 Jambonneau
11 Poitrine

Lamb Mouton

1 Côtes premières
2 Selle
3 Filet
4 Gigot
5 Haut de côtelettes
6 Côtes secondes
7 Côtes découvertes
8 Collier
9 Epaule
10 Poitrine

For steak, liver or kidneys, do as above:

Some steak, please	**Du biftek, s'il vous plaît**
	doo beeftek sil voo pleh
Some liver	**Du foie**
	doo fwah
Some kidneys	**Des rognons**
	deh ron-yon
Some heart	**Du cœur**
	doo ker
Some sausages	**Des saucisses**
	deh so-seess
Some mince . . .	**De la viande hachée**
	der lah vee-ahnd asheh
for three people	**pour trois personnes**
	poor trawh pair-son
for five people	**pour cinq personnes**
	poor san pair-son

For chops do it this way:

Two veal escalopes	**Deux escalopes de veau**
	der escalop der vo
Three pork chops	**Trois côtelettes de porc**
	trwah cotlet der por
Four lamb chops	**Quatre côtelettes d'agneau**
	kat cotlet dan-yo
Five mutton chops	**Cinq côtelettes de mouton**
	san cotlet der mooton

You may also want:

A chicken	**Un poulet**
	an pooleh
A rabbit	**Un lapin**
	an lah-pan
A tongue	**Une langue**
	oon lahng

Other essential expressions [*see also p. 54*]:

Other essential expressions [*see also p. 54*]:

Please can you . . .	**S'il vous plaît, pouvez-vous . . .**
	sil voo pleh, pooveh voo . . .
mince it?	**le hacher?**
	ler asheh
dice it?	**le découper en dés?**
	ler dehcoopeh ahn deh
trim the fat?	**enlever le gras?**
	ahnlerveh ler grah

Fish

ESSENTIAL INFORMATION

- The place to ask for:
  UNE POISSONNERIE (fish shop)
- Another key word to look for is **FRUITS DE MER** (seafood).
- Markets and large supermarkets usually have a fresh fish stall.
- Weight guide: 8 oz/250g minimum per person, for one meal of
  fish bought on the bone
  i.e. ½ kg/500 g   for 2 people
      1 kg   for 4 people
      1½ kg   for 6 people

WHAT TO SAY

Purchase large fish and small shellfish by weight:

½ kilo of ...	**Un demi-kilo de* ...**
	an der-me keelo der ...
1 kilo of ...	**Un kilo de* ...**
	an keelo der ...
1½ kilos of ...	**Un kilo et demi de* ...**
	an keelo eh der-me der ...
anchovies	**anchois**
	ahn-shwah
cod	**morue**
	moroo
eel	**anguille**
	ahn-gweel
mussels	**moules**
	mool
oysters	**huîtres**
	weet
prawns	**crevettes roses**
	crer-vet rose
red mullet	**rougets**
	roosheh

* Use **d'** in front of words beginning with a vowel.

1½ kilos of ...	**Un kilo et demi de ...**
	an keelo eh der-me der ...
sardines	**sardines**
	sardeen
shrimps	**crevettes grises**
	crer-vet greez
turbot	**turbot**
	toorbo
whiting	**merlans**
	mairlahn

Some large fish can be purchased by the slice:

One slice of ...	**Une tranche de ...**
	oon trahnsh der ...
Two slices of ...	**Deux tranches de ...**
	der trahnsh der ...
Six slices of ...	**Six tranches de ...**
	see trahnsh der ...
cod	**cabillaud**
	cahbee-yo
salmon	**saumon**
	somon
tuna (fresh)	**thon**
	ton

For some shellfish and 'frying pan' fish, specify the number you want:

A crab, please	**Un crabe, s'il vous plaît**
	an crab sil voo pleh
A herring	**Un hareng**
	an ah-rahn
A lobster	**Une langouste/Un homard**
	oon lahngoost/an omar
A mackerel	**Un maquereau**
	an mackro
A scallop	**Une coquille de Saint-Jacques**
	oon cokee der san shack
A sole	**Une sole**
	oon sol
A trout	**Une truite**
	oon trweet
A whiting	**Un merlan**
	an mairlahn

Other essential expressions [*see also p. 54*]:

Please can you ...	**S'il vous plaît, pouvez-vous ...**
	sil voo pleh pooveh voo ...
take the heads off?	**enlever les têtes?**
	ahnlerveh leh tet
clean them?	**les vider?**
	leh veedeh
fillet them?	**les découper en filets?**
	leh dehcoopeh ahn feeleh

Eating and drinking out

Ordering a drink

ESSENTIAL INFORMATION

- The places to ask for: [*see p. 18*]
  BAR
  CAFÉ
- The price list of drinks (**TARIF DES CONSOMMATIONS**) must, by law, be displayed outside or in the window.
- There is a waiter service in all cafés and bars, but you can drink at the bar or counter if you wish (cheaper).
- Always leave a tip of 10% or 15% of the bill unless you see **SERVICE COMPRIS** or **PRIX NETS** (service included) printed on the bill or on a notice.
- Bars and cafés serve both alcoholic and non-alcoholic drinks. There are no licensing laws and children are allowed in.

WHAT TO SAY

I'd like . . . please	**Je voudrais . . . s'il vous plaît**
	sher voodreh . . . sil voo pleh
a black coffee	**un café nature/un café noir**
	an cahfeh nahtoor/an cahfeh nwah
a coffee with cream	**un café crème**
	an cahfeh crem
a hot chocolate	**un chocolat chaud**
	an shocolah sho
a tea	**un thé**
	an teh
with milk	**au lait**
	o leh
with lemon	**au citron**
	o seetron
a Coca-Cola	**un Coca-Cola**
	an coca-cola
a glass of milk	**un verre de lait**
	an vair der leh

a lemonade	une limonade
	oon leemonad
a lemon squash	une citronnade
	oon seetronad
a mineral water	un Perrier
	an pair-yeh
an orangeade	une orangeade
	oon orahn-shad
an orange juice	un jus d'orange
	an shoo dorahnsh
a grape juice	un jus de raisin
	an shoo der rehzan
a pineapple juice	un jus d'ananas
	an shoo dahnahnah
a beer	une bière
	oon be-air
a draught beer	une bière pression
	oon be-air pressee-on
a light ale	une Kanterbrau
	oon Kanterbro
a lager	une Pils
	oon pils
a half	un demi
	an der-me
A glass of . . .	Un verre de . . .
	an vair der . . .
Two glasses of . . .	Deux verres de . . .
	der vair der . . .
red wine	vin rouge
	van roosh
white wine	vin blanc
	van blahn
rosé wine	vin rosé
	van roseh
dry	sec
	sek
sweet	doux
	doo
sparkling wine	vin mousseux
	van moosser
champagne	champagne
	shampan

A whisky	Un whisky
	an whisky
with ice	avec des glaçons
	ahvec deh glasson
with water	à l'eau
	ah lo
with soda	avec soda
	ahvec soda
A gin	Un gin
	an gin
and tonic	avec Schweppes
	ahvec shwep
with lemon	avec citron
	ahvec seetron
A brandy/cognac	Un cognac
	an cognac

These are local drinks you may like to try:

un Calvados	apple brandy
an calvados	
un citron pressé	freshly squeezed lemon drink
an seetron presseh	
un cointreau	orange liqueur (digestive)
an cwentro	
un diabolo-menthe	lemonade and mint cordial
an dee-ahbolo-mahnt	
une eau de vie	a type of brandy (digestive)
oon o der vee	
une infusion	herb tea (drunk after meals)
oon anfoozee-on	
un muscat	a sweet red wine (apéritif)
an moo-skah	
un Cazanis/un Ricard/un Pernod/un pastis	drink made from aniseed and brandy (apéritif)
an cazanis/an reecar/an pairno/ an pass-teess	

Other essential expressions:

Miss! [*this does not sound abrupt in French*]	**Mademoiselle!**
	mad-mwahzel
Waiter!	**Garçon!**
	gar-son
The bill, please!	**L'addition, s'il vous plaît!**
	laddisee-on sil voo pleh
How much does that come to?	**Ça fait combien?**
	sah feh combee-an
Is service included?	**Est-ce que le service est compris?**
	esk ler sairvees eh compree
Where is the toilet, please?	**Où sont les WC, s'il vous plaît?**
	oo son leh veh-seh sil voo pleh

Ordering a snack

ESSENTIAL INFORMATION

- Look for a café or bar with these signs: **CASSE-CROÛTE À TOUTE HEURE** (snacks at any time) and **SANDWICHS**
- Look for the names of snacks (listed below) on signs in the window or on the pavement.
- In some regions mobile vans sell hot snacks. ● For cakes, see p. 61.
- For ice-cream, see p. 63. ● For picnic-type snacks, see p. 68.

WHAT TO SAY

I'd like . . . please	**Je voudrais . . . s'il vous plaît** sher voodreh . . . sil voo pleh
a cheese sandwich	**un sandwich au fromage** an sandwich o fromash
a ham sandwich	**un sandwich au jambon** an sandwich o shahmbon
a pancake	**une crêpe** oon crep

These are some other snacks you may like to try:

une choucroûte garnie oon shoo-croot gahrnee	sauerkraut usually served with ham, smoked bacon and sausage
un croque-monsieur an crok-mer-see-er	toasted ham and cheese sandwich
des frites deh freet	chips
un hot-dog an ot-dog	a hot dog
un sandwich au saucisson an sandwich o so-see-son	a salami sandwich
un sandwich au pâté an sandwich o pah-teh	a pâté sandwich

Some snacks e.g. chips may be sold at a variety of prices. You should add to the order:

5/10 francs worth of chips	**Cinq/dix francs de frites** sank/dee frahn der freet

[*For other essential expressions, see 'Ordering a drink', p. 80.*]

In a restaurant

ESSENTIAL INFORMATION

- The place to ask for: **UN RESTAURANT** [*see p. 18.*]
- You can eat at these places:
  RESTAURANT
  CAFÉ
  BUFFET (at stations)
  ROUTIERS (transport cafés)
  BRASSERIE (limited choice here)
  RELAIS
  AUBERGE
  RÔTISSERIE
  DRUGSTORE
  BISTRO
  LIBRE-SERVICE (self-service cafeterias on the
  outskirts of towns or in hypermarkets)
- By law, the menus must be displayed outside or in the window –
  and that is the *only* way to judge if a place is right for your needs.
- Self-service restaurants are not unknown (see above), but all other
  places have waiter service.
- Leave a tip unless you see **SERVICE COMPRIS** on the bill or on
  the menu.
- Children's portions are not usually available.
- Eating times: usually from 11.30–2, and from 7–10, but these vary
  a great deal according to the type of establishment.

WHAT TO SAY

May I book a table?	**Puis-je réserver une table?**
	pweesh reh-zairveh oon tab
I've booked a table	**J'ai réservé une table**
	sheh reh-zairveh oon tab
A table ...	**Une table ...**
	oon tab ...
for one	**pour une personne**
	poor oon pair-son
for three	**pour trois personnes**
	poor trwah pair-son
The à la carte menu, please	**La carte, s'il vous plaît**
	la cart sil voo pleh

The fixed price menu	**Le menu à prix fixe** ler mer-noo ah pree fix
The 25 franc menu	**Le menu à vingt-cinq francs** ler mer-noo ah vant-san frahn
The tourist menu	**Le menu touristique** ler mer-noo touristeek
Today's special menu	**Le menu du jour** ler mer-noo doo shoor
The wine list	**La carte des vins** lah cart deh van
What's this, please? [*point to menu*]	**Qu'est ce que c'est ça, s'il vous plaît?** kesk seh sah sil voo pleh
A carafe of wine, please	**Une carafe de vin, s'il vous plaît** oon car-af der van sil voo pleh
A quarter (25 cc)	**Un quart** an car
A half (50 cc)	**Une demi-carafe** oon der-me car-af
A glass	**Un verre** an vair
A bottle/a litre	**Une bouteille/un litre** oon bootay/an leet
A half-bottle	**Une demi-bouteille** oon der-me bootay
Red/white/rosé/house wine	**Du vin rouge/blanc/rosé/maison** doo van roosh/blahn/roseh/mehzon
Some more bread, please	**Encore du pain, s'il vous plaît** ahncor doo pan sil voo pleh
Some more wine	**Encore du vin** ahncor doo van
Some oil	**De l'huile** der lweel
Some vinegar	**Du vinaigre** doo veeneg
Some salt	**Du sel** doo sel
Some pepper	**Du poivre** doo pwahv
Some water	**De l'eau** der lo
With/without (garlic)	**Sans/avec de (l'ail)** sahn/ahvec der (lie)

How much does that come to?	Ça fait combien?
	sah feh combee-an
Is service included?	Est-ce que le service est compris?
	esk ler sairvees eh compree
Where is the toilet, please?	Où sont les WC s'il vous plaît?
	oon son leh veh-seh sil voo pleh
Miss! [*this does not sound abrupt in French*]	Mademoiselle!
	mad-mwahzel
Waiter!	Garçon!
	gar-son
The bill, please	L'addition, s'il vous plaît
	laddisee-on sil voo pleh

Key words for courses, as seen on some menus: [*Only ask this question if you want the waiter to remind you of the choice.*]

What have you got in the way of . . .	Qu'est-ce que vous avez comme . . .
	kesk voozahveh com
starters?	hors d'œuvre?
	or derv
soup?	soupe?
	soup
egg dishes?	œufs?
	er
fish?	poisson?
	pwah-son
meat?	viande?
	vee-ahnd
game?	gibier?
	sheeb-yeh
fowl?	volaille?
	vol-eye
vegetables?	légumes?
	lehgoom
cheese?	fromages?
	fromash
fruit?	fruits?
	frwee
ice-cream?	glaces?
	glass
dessert?	dessert?
	deh-sair

UNDERSTANDING THE MENU

● You will find the names of the principal ingredients of most dishes on these pages:

Starters p. 68	Fruit p. 71
Meat p. 74	Cheese p. 70
Fish p. 77	Ice-cream p. 63
Vegetables p. 72	Dessert p. 61

Used together with the following lists of cooking and menu terms, they should help you to decode the menu.

● These cooking and menu terms are for understanding only – not for speaking.

Cooking and menu terms

à l'anglaise	boiled
au beurre	with butter
au beurre noir	fried in sizzling butter
bien cuit	well done
bisque	shellfish soup
blanquette	cooked in a creamy sauce
au bleu	boiled in water, oil and thyme (fish) very rare (meat)
bonne femme	baked with wine and vegetables
bouilli	boiled
braisé	braised
en broche	spit-roasted
en cocotte	stewed
coquilles	cooked in a white sauce and browned under the grill
en croûte	in a pastry case
en daube	braised in a wine stock
à l'étouffée	stewed
farci	stuffed
au four	baked
à la française	cooked with lettuce and onion
frit	fried
froid	cold
fumé	smoked
garni	served with vegetables or chips
au gratin	sprinkled with breadcrumbs and browned under the grill

grillé	grilled
haché	minced
maître d'hôtel	served with butter mixed with parsley and lemon juice
Marengo	cooked in oil, tomatoes and white wine
mousseline	mousse
Parmentier	containing potatoes
poché	poached
à point	medium
à la provençale	cooked with garlic, tomatoes, olive oil, olives, onions and herbs
rôti	roasted
saignant	rare
salade	served with oil and vinegar dressing
sauce béarnaise'	vinegar, egg yolks, white wine, butter, shallots and tarragon
sauce béchamel	flour, butter and milk
sauce bourguignonne	red wine sauce with herbs, onions and spices
sauce madère	cooked in Madeira wine
sauce Mornay	cheese sauce
sauce piquante	sharp vinegar sauce with chopped gherkins and herbs
sauté	fried slowly in butter
en terrine	preparation of meat, game or fowl baked in a terrine (casserole) and served cold
à la vapeur	steamed
Vichy	garnished with carrots
vinaigrette	with oil and vinegar dressing

Further words to help you understand the menu

assiette anglaise	cold meat and salad
boudin	black pudding
bouillabaisse	rich fish soup in which a variety of fish and shell fish have been cooked. Soup and fish are served in separate dishes
champignons	mushrooms
chantilly	cream whipped with icing sugar

choucroûte	sauerkraut
compote	stewed fruit
consommé	clear broth
crudités	raw vegetables and salads served as starters
cuisses de grenouilles	frogs' legs
escalopes panées	veal escalopes fried in egg and breadcrumbs
escargots	snails
flan	egg custard
moules	mussels
potage	vegetable soup
quenelles	fish or meat fingers cooked in a white sauce
ragoût	stew
ratatouille	a vegetable stew
ris de veau	veal sweetbreads
sorbet	water ice
tournedos	fillet steak

Health

ESSENTIAL INFORMATION

- For details of reciprocal health agreements between your country and the country you are visiting, visit your local Department of Health office at least one month before leaving, or ask your travel agent.
- In addition, it is preferable to purchase a medical insurance policy through the travel agent, a broker or a motoring organization.
- Take your own 'first line' first aid kit with you.
- For minor disorders and treatment at a drug store, see p. 40.
- For finding your way to a doctor, dentist, drug store or Health and Social Security Office (for reimbursement), see p. 18.
- Once in France decide a definite plan of action in case of serious illness: communicate your problem to a near neighbour, the receptionist or someone you see regularly. You are then dependent on that person helping you obtain treatment.
- To find a doctor in an emergency, look for:
  Médecins (in the Yellow Pages of the telephone directory)
  Les Urgences (casualty department)
  H
  Hôpital } (hospital)

What's the matter?

I have a pain ...	J'ai mal ...
	sheh mal ...
in my abdomen	au ventre
	o vahnt
in my ankle	à la cheville
	ah lah sher-vee
in my arm	au bras
	o bra
in my back	au dos
	o doh
in my bladder	à la vessie
	ah lah vessee
in my bowels	à l'intestin
	ah lantestan

I have a pain . . .	J'ai mal . . .
	sheh mal . . .
in my breast	au sein
	o san
in my chest	à la poitrine
	ah lah pwahtreen
in my ear	à l'oreille
	ah loray
in my eye	à l'œil
	ah ler-yer
in my foot	au pied
	o pee-eh
in my head	à la tête
	ah lah tet
in my heel	au talon
	o tah-lon
in my jaw	à la mâchoire
	ah lah mah-shwah
in my kidney	au rein
	o ran
in my leg	à la jambe
	ah lah shahmb
in my lung	au poumon
	o poomon
in my neck	au cou
	o coo
in my penis	au pénis
	o penneess
in my shoulder	à l'épaule
	ah lehpol
in my stomach	à l'estomac
	ah lestomah
in my testicle	au testicule
	o testicool
in my throat	à la gorge
	ah lah gorsh
in my vagina	au vagin
	o vah-shan
in my wrist	au poignet
	o pwah-nee-eh
I have a pain here [*point*]	J'ai mal ici
	sheh mal ee-see

I have a toothache	**J'ai mal aux dents** sheh mal o dahn
I have broken ...	**J'ai cassé ...** sheh casseh ...
my dentures	**mon dentier** mon dahnt-yeh
my glasses	**mes lunettes** meh loonet
I have lost ...	**J'ai perdu ...** sheh pairdoo ...
my contact lenses	**mes verres de contact** meh vair der contact
a filling	**un plombage** an plombash
My child is ill	**Mon enfant est malade** mon ahnfahn eh mal-ad
He/she has a pain in his/ her ... ankle [see list above]	**Il/elle a mal ...*** il/el ah mal ... à la cheville ah lah sher-vee
How bad is it?	
I'm ill	**Je suis malade** sher swee mal-ad
It's urgent	**C'est urgent** set oorshahn
It's serious	**C'est grave** seh grav
It's not serious	**Ce n'est pas grave** ser neh pah grav
It hurts	**Ça me fait mal** sah mer feh mal
It hurts a lot	**Ça me fait très mal** sah mer feh treh mal
It doesn't hurt much	**Ça ne me fait pas très mal** sah ner mer feh pah treh mal
The pain occurs ...	**La douleur revient ...** lah dooler rer-vee-an ...
every quarter of an hour	**tous les quarts d'heure** too leh car der

*For boys use 'il', for girls use 'elle'.

The pain occurs ...	**La douleur revient ...**
	lah dooler rer-vee-an ...
every half hour	**toutes les demi-heures**
	toot leh der-me-er
every hour	**toutes les heures**
	toot leh zer
every day	**tous les jours**
	too leh shoor
It hurts most of the time	**C'est une douleur continue**
	set-oon dooler conteenoo
I've had it for ...	**Ça me fait mal depuis ...**
	sah mer feh mal der-pwee ...
one hour/one day	**une heure/un jour**
	ooner/an shoor
two hours/two days	**deux heures/deux jours**
	der-zer/der shoor
It's a ...	**C'est une ...**
	set oon ...
sharp pain	**douleur aiguë**
	dooler eggoo
dull ache	**douleur sourde**
	dooler soord
nagging pain	**douleur irritante**
	dooler irritahnt
I feel ...	**J'ai ...**
	sheh ...
dizzy	**des vertiges**
	deh vairteesh
sick	**la nausée**
	lah nozeh
I feel ...	**Je me sens ...**
	sher mer sahn ...
weak	**faible**
	feb
feverish	**fiévreux/fiévreuse***
	fee-evrer/fee-evrerz

Already under treatment for something else?

I take ... regularly [*show*]	**Je prends ... régulièrement**
	sher prahn ... rehgool-yair-mahn

* Men use the first alternative, women the second.

this medicine	ce médicament
	ser meh-deecah-**mahn**
these pills	ces pilules
	seh peelool
I have . . .	**J'ai . . .**
	sheh . . .
a heart condition	le cœur malade
	ler ker mal-ad
haemorrhoids	des hémorroïdes
	deh zeh-moro-eed
rheumatism	des rhumatismes
	deh rheumateesm
I am . . .	**Je suis . . .**
	sher swee . . .
diabetic	diabétique
	dee-ah-beh-teek
asthmatic	asthmatique
	asthmateek
pregnant	enceinte
	ahn-sant
allergic to (penicillin)	allergique à (la pénicilline)
	allersheek ah (lah penicillin)

Other essential expressions

Please can you help?	Pouvez-vous m'aider s'il vous plaît?
	pooveh-voo med-eh sil voo pleh
A doctor, please	Un docteur, s'il vous plaît
	an doc-ter sil voo pleh
A dentist	Un dentiste
	an dahnteest
I don't speak French	Je ne parle pas français
	sher ner parl pah frahn-seh
What time does . . . arrive?	A quelle heure arrive . . .
	ah keller ahreev . . .
the doctor	le docteur?
	ler doc-ter
the dentist	le dentiste?
	ler dahntist

From the doctor: key sentences to understand

Take this ...	Prenez ceci ...
	prer-neh ser-see ...
every day	tous les jours
	too leh shoor
every hour	toutes les heures
	toot leh zer
four times a day	quatre fois par jour
	kat fwah par shoor
Stay in bed	Gardez le lit
	gardeh ler lee
Don't travel ...	Ne voyagez pas ...
	ner vwah-yah-sheh pah ...
for ... days/weeks	avant ... jours/semaines
	ahvahn ... shoor/ser-men
You must go to hospital	Vous devez aller à l'hôpital
	voo der-veh ahleh ah lopetal

Problems: complaints, loss, theft

ESSENTIAL INFORMATION

- Problems with:
  camping facilities, see p. 34;
  household appliances, see p. 52;
  health, see p. 91;
  the car, see p. 106.
- If the worst comes to the worst, find the police station. To ask the
  way, see p. 18.
- Look for:
  GENDARMERIE (police)
  COMMISSARIAT DE POLICE (police station)
- If you lose your passport report the loss to the police and go to the
  nearest consulate of your country.
- In an emergency, dial 17 for police/ambulance and 18 for the fire
  brigade.

COMPLAINTS

I bought this . . .	J'ai acheté ça . . . sheh ashtch sah . . .
today	aujourd'hui o-shoordwee
yesterday	hier ee-air
on Monday [see p. 130]	lundi lerndee
It's no good (not suitable)	Ça ne va pas sah ner vah pah
It's no good (faulty)	Il y a un défaut il yah an dehfo
Look	Regardez rer-gardeh
Here [point]	Ici ee-see

Can you . . .	**Pouvez-vous . . .**
	pooveh-voo . . .
change it ?	**l'échanger?**
	leh-shahn-sheh
mend it ?	**le réparer?**
	ler reh-pah-reh
give me a refund ?	**me rembourser?**
	mer rahmboor-seh
Here's the receipt	**Voici le reçu**
	vwah-see ler rer-soo
Can I see the manager ?	**Puis-je voir le directeur?**
	pweesh vwah ler deerecter

LOSS
[*See also 'Theft' below: the lists are interchangeable*]

I have lost . . .	**J'ai perdu . . .**
	sheh pairdoo . . .
my bag	**mon sac**
	mon sac
my bracelet	**mon bracelet**
	mon brassleh
my camera	**mon appareil photo**
	mon appah-ray photo
my car keys	**les clés de ma voiture**
	leh cleh der mah vwahtoor
my car logbook	**ma carte grise**
	mah cart greez
my driving licence	**mon permis de conduire**
	mon pairmee der condweer
my insurance certificate	**mon assurance**
	mon assoorahns
my jewellery	**mes bijoux**
	meh bee-shoo
I have lost everything!	**J'ai tout perdu!**
	sheh too pairdoo

THEFT
[*See also 'Loss' above: the lists are interchangeable.*]

Someone has stolen . . .	**On m'a volé . . .**
	on mah voleh . . .
my car	**ma voiture**
	mah vwahtoor

my car radio	mon autoradio
	mon autorah-dio
my keys	mes clés
	meh cleh
my money	mon argent
	mon arshahn
my necklace	mon collier
	mon col-yeh
my passport	mon passeport
	mon passpor
my radio	mon transistor
	mon transistor
my tickets	mes billets
	meh bee-yeh
my travellers' cheques	mes traveller chèques
	meh traveller shek
my wallet	mon portefeuille
	mon port-fey
my watch	ma montre
	mah mont
my luggage	mes bagages
	meh baggash

LIKELY REACTIONS: key words to understand

Wait	Attendez
	attahndeh
When?	Quand?
	kahn
Where?	Où?
	oo
Name?	Nom?
	nom
Address?	Adresse?
	address
I can't help you	Je ne puis rien pour vous
	sher ner pwee ree-an poor voo
Nothing to do with me	Ce n'est pas ici qu'il faut s'adresser
	ser neh pah ee-see kil fo saddresseh

The post office

ESSENTIAL INFORMATION

- To find a post office, see p. 18.
- Key words to look for:
  POSTES
  POSTE, TÉLÉGRAPHE, TÉLÉPHONE (PTT)
  POSTES ET TÉLÉCOMMUNICATIONS (PT)
- Look for this sign:

POSTES
TELECOMMUNICATIONS

- It is best to buy stamps at the smoke shop.
  Only go to the post office for more complicated
  transactions, like telegrams.
- Look for these signs on the shop.
- Letter boxes are yellow (red in Belgium).
- For poste restante you should show your
  passport at the counter marked **POSTE
  RESTANTE** in the main post office, and pay
  a small charge.

WHAT TO SAY

To England, please

Pour l'Angleterre, s'il vous plaît
poor lahng-tair sil voo pleh

[*Hand letters, cards or parcels over the counter.*]

To Australia

Pour l'Australie
poor lostrah-lee

To the United States

Pour les États-Unis
poor leh zehtah-zoonee

[*For other countries, see p. 134.*]

How much is ...

C'est combien ...
seh combee-an ...

this parcel (to Canada)?

ce colis (pour le Canada)?
ser collee (poor ler canada)

a letter (to Australia)?

une lettre (pour l'Australie)?
oon let (poor lostrah-lee)

a postcard (to England)?

une carte postale (pour l'Angleterre)?
oon cart postahl (poor lahng-tair)

Air mail

Par avion
par ahvee-on

Surface mail

Ordinaire
ordeenair

One stamp, please

Un timbre, s'il vous plaît
an tamb sil voo pleh

Two stamps

Deux timbres
der tamb

One (1F 50) stamp

Un timbre à (un franc cinquante)
an tamb ah (an frahn sankahnt)

I'd like to send a telegram

Je voudrais envoyer un télégramme
sher voodreh ahn-vwah-yeh an
    telegram

Telephoning

ESSENTIAL INFORMATION

- Unless you read and speak French well, it's best not to make phone calls by yourself. Go to the main post office and write the town and number you want on a piece of paper. Add **avec préavis** if you want a person-to-person call or **PCV** if you want to reverse the charges.
- Public phones are located in perspex kiosks.
- To ask the way to a public phone, see p. 18.
- To make a call from an automatic public phone:
  put the appropriate coins in the slot. Life the receiver. Wait for dial tone. Dial. Put in more money when the sign **Épuisé** lights up.
- To call the operator, dial 10, but you have to pay!
- To make a call from a café you will have to buy a **jeton** (sold in cafés and post offices) to use instead of a coin. As above, insert the **jeton** and wait for a dialling tone.
- For international calls dial 19. Wait for second buzzing noise and then dial 44 for Great Britain (and London) or 1 for the United States. Then dial the town/area code number and the subscriber's number.

WHAT TO SAY

Where can I make a telephone call?	**Où puis-je téléphoner?** oo pweesh telephoneh
Local/abroad	**Dans la région/à l'étranger** dahn lah resh-yon/ah lettrahn-sheh
I'd like this number ... [show number]	**Je voudrais ce numéro ...** sher voodreh ser noomehro ...
in England	**en Angleterre** ahn ahng-tair
in Canada	**au Canada** o canada
in the USA	**aux États-Unis** o zehtah- zoonee

[For other countries, see p. 134.]

Can you dial it for me, please?
Pouvez-vous me l'appeler, s'il vous plaît?
poveh-voo mer lap-leh sil voo pleb

How much is it?
C'est combien?
seh combee-an

Hello!
Allô!
allo

May I speak to ... ?
Puis-je parler à ... ?
pweesh parleh ah ...

Extension ...
Poste ...
post ...

I'm sorry, I don't speak French
Je regrette, je ne parle pas français
sher rer-gret sher ner parl pah frahn-seh

Do you speak English?
Parlez-vous anglais?
parleh-voo ahngleh

Thank you. I'll phone back
Merci. Je rappellerai
mair-see sher rappel-reh

Goodbye
Au revoir
o rer-vwah

LIKELY REACTIONS

That's 4 francs 50
Ça fait quatre francs cinquante
sah feh kat frahn sankahnt

Cabin number (3)
Cabine numéro (trois)
cabin noomehro (trwah)

[*For numbers, see p. 126.*]

Don't hang up
Ne quittez pas
ner keeteh pah

I'm trying to connect you
J'essaie de vous passer l'abonné
shesseh de voo pah-seh lahboneh

You're through
Parlez
parleh

There's a delay
Il y a une attente
il yah oon attahnt

I'll try again
J'essaie encore (une fois)
shesseh ahncor (oon fwah)

Changing checks and money

ESSENTIAL INFORMATION

- Finding your way to a bank or change bureau, see p. 18.
- Look for these words on buildings:
  BANQUE
  CRÉDIT
  SOCIÉTÉ GÉNÉRALE
  BUREAU DE CHANGE
  CHANGE
- To cash your normal checks, exactly as at home, use your credit card where you see the Eurocheque sign. Write in English.
- Have your passport handy.

WHAT TO SAY

I'd like to cash ...	Je voudrais encaisser ...
	sher voodreh ahn-kesseh ...
this travellers' cheque	ce traveller chèque
	ser traveller shek
these travellers' cheques	ces traveller chèques
	seh traveller shek
this cheque	ce chèque
	ser shek
I'd like to change this into French francs	Je voudrais changer ceci en francs français
	sher voodreh shan-sheh ser-see ahn frahn frahn-seh
Here's ...	Voici ...
	vwah-see ...
my banker's card	ma carte
	mah cart
my passport	mon passeport
	mon passpor

For excursions into neighbouring countries

I'd like to change this . . .	**Je voudrais changer ceci . . .**
[*show bank notes*]	sher voodreh shahn-sheh **ser-see . . .**
into Austrian schillings	**en schillings autrichiens**
	ahn shilling otreesh-**yan**
into Belgian francs	**en francs belges**
	ahn frahn belsh
into German marks	**en marks**
	ahn mark
into Italian lira	**en lires**
	ahn leer
into Spanish pesetas	**en pesetas**
	ahn pesetas
into Swiss francs	**en francs suisses**
	ahn frahn sweess
What's the rate of exchange?	**Quel est le taux de change?**
	kelleh ler to der shahnsh

LIKELY REACTIONS

Passport, please	**Passeport, s'il vous plaît**
	passpor sil voo pleh
Sign here	**Signez ici**
	seen-yeh ee-see
Your banker's card, please	**Votre carte, s'il vous plaît**
	vot cart sil voo pleh
Go to the cash desk	**Passez à la caisse**
	passeh ah lah kess

Car travel

ESSENTIAL INFORMATION

- Finding a filling station or garage, see p. 18.
- Is it a self-service station? Look out for **LIBRE SERVICE** or **SERVEZ-VOUS**.
- Grades of gasoline:

  NORMALE
  ORDINAIRE } (2 star, standard)
  SUPER (CARBURANT) (3 star and above, premium)
  GAS-OIL (diesel)
- 1 gallon is about 4½ litres (accurate enough up to 6 gallons).
- for car repairs, look for:

  DÉPANNAGE (repairs)
  GARAGE (garage)
  MÉCANICIEN (mechanic)
  CARROSSERIE (for body work)
- Gas stations outside towns will sometimes close from 12-3.
- In the case of a breakdown or an emergency look for the **TCF** (French Touring Club) sign, or dial 6969 (**Touring Secours**) from any telephone box.
- Unfamiliar road signs and warnings, see p. 121.

WHAT TO SAY
[*For numbers, see p. 126.*]

(Nine) litres	(Neuf) litres
	(nerf) leet
(Two hundred) francs	(Deux cents) francs
	(der sahn) frahn
of standard	d'ordinaire
	dordeenair
of premium	de super
	der soopair
of diesel	de gas-oil
	der gazwahl
Fill it up, please	Faites le plein, s'il vous plaît
	fet ler plan sil voo pleh

Can you check . . .   **Pouvez-vous vérifier . . .**
pooveh voo vehrif-yeh . . .

   the oil?   **l'huile?**
lweel

   the battery?   **la batterie?**
lah battree

   the radiator?   **le radiateur?**
ler raddee-atter

   the tyres?   **les pneus?**
leh pner

I've run out of petrol   **Je suis en panne d'essence**
sher swee ahn pan dessahns

Can I borrow a can, please?   **Puis-je emprunter un bidon s'il
vous plaît?**
pweesh ahmprernteh an beedon sil
voo pleh

My car has broken down   **Ma voiture est en panne**
mah vwahtoor eh ahn pan

My car won't start   **Ma voiture ne démarre pas**
mah vwahtoor ner deh-mar pah

I've had an accident   **J'ai eu un accident**
sheh oo an accidahn

I've lost my car keys   **J'ai perdu les clés de ma voiture**
sheh pairdoo leh cleh der mah
vwahtoor

My car is . . .   **Ma voiture est . . .**
mah vwahtoor eh . . .

   two kilometres away   **à deux kilomètres**
ah der keelomet

   three kilometres away   **à trois kilomètres**
ah trwah keelomet

Can you help me, please?   **Pouvez-vous m'aider, s'il vous plaît?**
pooveh voo med-eh sil voo pleh

Do you do repairs?   **Est-ce que vous faites les réparations?**
esk voo fet leh rehpahrah-see-on

I have a puncture   **J'ai une crevaison**
sheh oon crer-veh-zon

I have a broken windscreen   **Mon pare-brise est cassé**
mon par-breez eh casseh

I think the problem is
here . . . [point]   **Je crois que c'est ça qui ne va pas . . .**
sher crwah ker seh sah kee ner vah
pah . . .

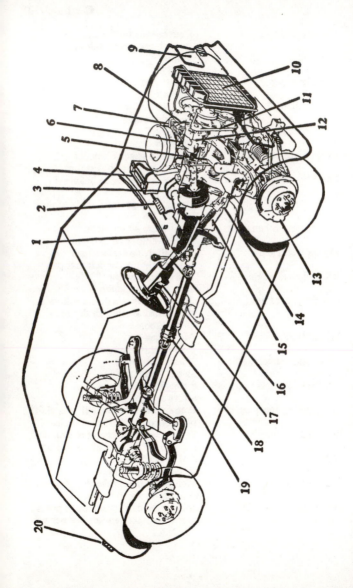

1 windscreen wipers	essuie-glace	eswee-glass
2 fuses	fusibles	foozeeb
3 heater	chauffage	shofash
4 battery	batterie	battree
5 engine	moteur	motor
6 fuel pump	pompe à essence	pomp ah essahns
7 starter motor	démarreur	dehmah-rer
8 carburettor	carburateur	carbooratter
9 lights	phares	far
10 radiator	radiateur	raddee-atter
11 fan belt	courroie de ventilation	coorwah der vahnteelah-see-on
12 generator	générateur	shehneh-ratter
13 brakes	freins	fran
14 clutch	embrayage	ahmbreh-yash
15 gear box	boîte à vitesses	bwaht ah veetess
16 steering	direction	deerec-see-on
17 ignition	allumage	alloomash
18 transmission	transmission	trahnsme-see-on
19 exhaust	tuyau d'échappement	twee-yo dehshap-mahn
20 indicators	clignotants	cleen-yotahn

I don't know what's wrong	**Je ne sais pas ce qui ne va pas**
	sher ner say pah ser kee ner vah pah
Can you ...	**Pouvez-vous ...**
	pooveh-voo ...
repair the fault?	**faire la réparation?**
	fair lah reh-pahrah-see-on
come and look?	**venir voir?**
	ver-neer vwah
estimate the cost?	**me donner un prix?**
	mer donneh an pree
write it down?	**l'écrire?**
	lehcreer
Do you accept these coupons?	**Acceptez-vous ces coupons?**
	accepteh-voo seh coopon
How long will the repair take?	**Combien de temps prendra la réparation?**
	combee-an der tahn prahndrah lah rehpahrah-see-on
When will the car be ready?	**La voiture sera prête quand?**
	lah vwahtoor ser-rah pret kahn
Can I see the bill?	**Puis-je voir la note?**
	pweesh vwah lah not
This is my insurance document	**Voici mon assurance**
	vwah-see mon assoorahns

HIRING A CAR

Can I hire a car?	**Puis-je louer une voiture?**
	pweesh loo-eh oon vwahtoor
I need a car ...	**J'ai besoin d'une voiture ...**
	sheh ber-zwan doon vwahtoor ...
for two people	**pour deux personnes**
	poor der pair-son
for five people	**pour cinq personnes**
	poor san pair-son
for one day	**pour une journée**
	poor oon shoorneh
for five days	**pour cinq jours**
	poor san shoor
for a week	**pour une semaine**
	poor oon ser-men

Can you write down . . .	**Pouvez-vous écrire . . .**
	pooveh-voo ehcreer . . .
the deposit to pay?	**les arrhes à verser?**
	leh zar ah vair-seh
the charge per kilometre?	**le tarif au kilomètre?**
	ler tariff o keelomet
the daily charge?	**le tarif à la journée?**
	ler tariff ah lah shoorneh
the cost of insurance?	**le montant de l'assurance?**
	ler montahn der lassoorahns
Can I leave it in (Paris)?	**Puis-je la laisser à (Paris)?**
	pweesh lah lesseh ah (pahree)
What documents do I need?	**Quels papiers me faut-il?**
	kel pap-yeh mer fo-til

LIKELY REACTIONS

I don't do repairs	**Je ne fais pas les réparations**
	sher ner feh-pah leh rehpahrahsee-on
Where's your car?	**Où est votre voiture?**
	oo eh vot vwahtoor
What make is it?	**C'est quelle marque?**
	seh kel mark
Come back tomorrow/on Monday	**Revenez demain/lundi**
	rer-venneh der-man/lerndee

[*For days of the week, see p. 130.*]

We don't hire cars	**On ne fait pas la location**
	on ner feh pah lah locah-see-on
Your driving licence, please	**Votre permis, s'il vous plaît**
	vot pairmee sil voo pleh
The mileage is unlimited	**Le kilométrage n'est pas limité**
	ler keelomeh-trash neh pah limiteh

Public transport

ESSENTIAL INFORMATION

- Finding the way to the bus station, bus stop, trolley stop, railway station and taxi stand, see p. 18.
- Remember that lining up for buses is unheard of!
- Taxis can be found at taxi stands in the main areas of a town, especially at the railway station.
- These are the different types of trains, graded according to speed (slowest to fastest):

  EXPRESS

  RAPIDE (a supplement is sometimes payable if the train is an exceptionally fast one)

  CORAIL (rolling stock: air-conditioned inter-city luxury train)

  TRANS EUROP EXPRESS (TEE) (first class only, supplement payable on these trains)
- Key words on signs [*see also p. 121*]:

  ACCÈS AUX QUAIS (to the trains)

  ARRÊT D'AUTOBUS (bus stop)

  BILLETS (tickets, ticket office)

  CONSIGNE (left luggage)

  ENTRÉE (entrance)

  HORAIRE (timetable)

  INTERDIT(E) (forbidden)

  LOCATIONS (bookings)

  MONTÉE (entrance for buses)

  N'OUBLIEZ PAS DE COMPOSTER (don't forget to validate)

  RENSEIGNEMENTS (information)

  QUAI (platform)

  SORTIE (exit)

  VOIE (platform)
- As French Railways have abolished ticket control at platform barriers, *you* must validate your ticket by using one of the orange-coloured date stamping machines provided at platform entrances *before* departure. If you fail to do so, you will be liable to a fine of up to 20% of your fare. Keep an eye out for the sign shown on the opposite page.

Accès aux quais **Au-delà de cette limite votre billet doit être valide compostez-le**

However, these regulations do not apply to international tickets purchased outside France.
- There is a flat rate for underground tickets and it is cheaper to buy **a carnet** (a book of ten tickets). In Paris, bus and underground tickets are interchangeable.
- Children under 10 pay half-fare on trains.

WHAT TO SAY

Where does the train for (Paris) leave from?
De quelle voie part le train de (Paris)?
der kel vwah par ler tran der (pahree)

At what time does the train leave for (Paris)?
A quelle heure part le train de (Paris)?
a keller par ler tran der (pahree)

At what time does the train arrive in (Paris)
A quelle heure le train arrive-t-il à (Paris)?
ah keller ler tran ahreev-til ah (pahree)

Is this the train for (Paris)?
Est-ce le train de (Paris)?
ess ler tran der (pahree)

Where does the bus for (Toulouse) leave from?
D'où part l'autobus de (Toulouse)?
doo par lotoboos der (too-looz)

At what time does the bus leave for (Toulouse)?
A quelle heure part l'autobus de (Toulouse)?
ah keller par lotoboos der (too-looz)

At what time does the bus arrive in (Toulouse)?
A quelle heure l'autobus arrive-t-il à (Toulouse)?
ah keller lotoboos ahreev-til ah (too-looz)

Is this the bus for (Toulouse)?
Est-ce l'autobus de (Toulouse)?
ess lotoboos der (too-looz)

Do I have to change?
Faut-il changer?
fo-til shahn-sheh

Where does . . . leave from?	D'où part . . .?
	doo par
the bus	l'autobus
	lotoboos
the train	le train
	ler tran
the underground	le métro
	ler metro
the boat/ferry	le bateau/le ferry
	ler bahto/ler ferry
for the airport	pour l'aéroport
	poor lah-ehropor
for the beach	pour la plage
	poor lah plash
for the cathedral	pour la cathédrale
	poor lah cattedrahl
for the market place	pour la place du marché
	poor lah plass doo marsheh
for the railway station	pour la gare
	poor lah gar
for St John's Church	pour l'église St Jean
	poor leh-gleez san-shahn
for the swimming pool	pour la piscine
	poor lah pee-seen
for the town centre	pour le centre de la ville
	poor ler sahnt der lah veel
for the town hall	pour la mairie
	poor lah meh-ree
Is this . . .	Est-ce . . .
	ess . . .
the bus for the market place?	l'autobus pour la place du marché?
	lotoboos poor lah plass doo marsheh
the tram for the railway station?	le tram pour la gare?
	ler tram poor lah gar
Where can I get a taxi?	Où puis-je trouver un taxi?
	oo pweesh trooveh an taxee
Can you put me off at the right stop, please?	Pouvez-vous me dire où je dois descendre?
	pooveh-voo mer deer oo sher dwah dessahnd
Can I book a seat?	Puis-je réserver une place?
	pweesh reh-zairveh oon plass

A single	**Un aller**
	an alleh
A return	**Un aller-retour**
	an alleh rer-toor
First class	**Première classe**
	prem-yair class
Second class	**Deuxième classe**
	der-zee-em class
One adult	**Un adulte**
	an ahdoolt
Two adults	**Deux adultes**
	der zahdoolt
and one child	**et un enfant**
	eh an ahnfahn
and two children	**et deux enfants**
	eh der zahnfahn
How much is it?	**C'est combien?**
	seh combee-an

LIKELY REACTIONS

Over there	**Là-bas**
	lah-bah
Here	**Ici**
	ee-see
Platform (1)	**Quai numéro (un)/(Première) voie**
	keh noomehro (an)/(prem-yair)
	vwah
At (4 o'clock)	**A (quatre heures)**
[*For times, see p. 128.*]	ah (kat er)
Change at (Vichy)	**Changez à (Vichy)**
	shahn-sheh ah (vee-she)
Change at (the town hall)	**Changez à (la mairie)**
	shahn-sheh ah (lah mairee)
This is your stop	**Voici votre arrêt**
	vwah-see vot ah-reh
There's only first class	**Il n'y a que des premières (classes)**
	il nee yah ker deh prem-yair (class)
There's a supplement	**Il y a un supplément**
	il yah an soopplehmahn

Leisure

ESSENTIAL INFORMATION

- Finding the way to a place of entertainment, see p. 18.
- For times of day, see p. 128.
- Important signs, see p. 121.
- In the more popular seaside resorts you have to pay to go on the beach and to rent deckchairs and umbrellas.
- Smoking is forbidden in movies and theatres, unless otherwise specified.
- You should tip theatre usherettes.

WHAT TO SAY

At what time does...open?	**A quelle heure ouvre ... ?**
	ah keller oov ...
the art gallery	**le musée d'art**
	ler moozeh dar
the botanical garden	**le jardin botanique**
	ler shardan botaneek
the cinema	**le cinéma**
	ler cinema
the concert hall	**la salle de concerts**
	lah sal der con-sair
the disco	**la discothèque**
	la discotek
the museum	**le musée**
	ler moozeh
the night club	**la boîte de nuit**
	lah bwaht der nwee
the sports stadium	**le stade**
	ler stad
the swimming pool	**la piscine**
	lah pee-seen
the theatre	**le théâtre**
	ler teh-art
the zoo	**le zoo**
	ler zo-o

At what time does . . . close?　　**A quelle heure ferme . . . ?**
　　　　　　　　　　　　　　　　ah keller fairm . . .

　the art gallery　　　　　　　　**le musée d'art**
　[*see above list*]　　　　　　　ler moozeh dar

At what time does . . . start?　　**A quelle heure commence . . . ?**
　　　　　　　　　　　　　　　　ah keller commahns . . .

　the cabaret　　　　　　　　　**le cabaret**
　　　　　　　　　　　　　　　ler cabaret

　the concert　　　　　　　　　**le concert**
　　　　　　　　　　　　　　　ler con-sair

　the film　　　　　　　　　　**le film**
　　　　　　　　　　　　　　　ler film

　the match　　　　　　　　　**le match**
　　　　　　　　　　　　　　　ler match

　the play　　　　　　　　　　**la pièce**
　　　　　　　　　　　　　　　lah pee-ess

　the race　　　　　　　　　　**la course**
　　　　　　　　　　　　　　　lah coorss

How much is it . . .　　　　　**C'est combien . . .**
　　　　　　　　　　　　　　　seh combee-an . . .

　for an adult?　　　　　　　　**pour un adulte?**
　　　　　　　　　　　　　　　poor an ahdoolt

　for a child?　　　　　　　　　**pour un enfant?**
　　　　　　　　　　　　　　　poor an ahnfahn

Two adults, please　　　　　　**Deux adultes, s'il vous plaît**
　　　　　　　　　　　　　　　der zahdoolt sil voo pleh

Three children, please　　　　　**Trois enfants, s'il vous plaît**
　　　　　　　　　　　　　　　trwah zahnfahn sil voo pleh

[*state price, if there is a choice*]
Stalls/circle/sun/shade　　　　　**Orchestre/balcon/au soleil/à l'ombre**
　　　　　　　　　　　　　　　orkest/balcon/o solay/ah lomb

Do you have . . .　　　　　　**Avez-vous . . .**
　　　　　　　　　　　　　　　ahveh-voo . . .

　a programme?　　　　　　　　**un programme?**
　　　　　　　　　　　　　　　an program

　a guide book?　　　　　　　　**un guide?**
　　　　　　　　　　　　　　　an gheed

Where is the toilet, please?　　　**Où sont les WC, s'il vous plaît?**
　　　　　　　　　　　　　　　oo son leh veh-seh sil voo pleh

Where's the cloakroom?　　　　**Où est le vestiaire?**
　　　　　　　　　　　　　　　oo eh ler vestee-air

I would like lessons in ...	**Je voudrais des leçons de ...**
	sher voodreh deh ler-son der ...
sailing	**voile**
	vwahl
skiing	**ski**
	skee
sub-aqua diving	**plongée sous-marine**
	plonsheh soo-marine
water skiing	**ski nautique**
	skee noteek
Can I hire ...	**Puis-je louer ...**
	pweesh loo-eh ...
some skis?	**des skis?**
	deh skee
some skiboots?	**des chaussures de ski?**
	deh shossooer der skee
a boat?	**un bateau?**
	an bahto
a fishing rod?	**une canne à pêche?**
	oon can ah pesh
a deckchair?	**une chaise-longue?**
	oon shez-long
a sun umbrella?	**un parasol?**
	an parasol
the necessary equipment?	**le nécessaire?**
	ler nesseh-sair
How much is it ...	**C'est combien ...**
	seh combee-an ...
per day/per hour?	**par jour/de l'heure?**
	par shoor/der ler
Must I have a licence?	**Faut-il un permis?**
	fo-til an pairmee

Asking if things are allowed

ESSENTIAL INFORMATION

● May one smoke here?
May we smoke here?
May I smoke here?
Can one smoke here?
Can we smoke here?
Can I smoke here?

On peut fumer ici?

● All these English variations can be expressed in one way in French. To save space, only the first English version (May one . . .?) is shown below.

WHAT TO SAY

Excuse me, please	**Excusez-moi**
	excooseh mwah
May one . . .	**On peut . . .**
	on per . . .
camp here?	**camper ici?**
	campeh ee-see
come in?	**entrer?**
	ahntreh
dance here?	**danser ici?**
	dahn seh ee-see
fish here?	**pêcher ici?**
	peh-sheh ee-see
get a drink here?	**avoir des boissons ici?**
	ahvwah deh bwah-son ee-see
get out this way?	**sortir par ici?**
	sorteer par ee-see
get something to eat here?	**manger quelque chose ici?**
	mahnsheh kelker shoz ee-see
leave one's things here?	**laisser ses affaires ici?**
	lesseh seh-zaffair ee-see
look around?	**regarder?**
	rer-gardeh
park here?	**se garer ici?**
	ser gahreh ee-see

May one ...	On peut ... on per ...
picnic here?	**pique-niquer ici?** peek-neekeh ee-see
sit here?	**s'asseoir ici?** sasswah ee-see
smoke here?	**fumer ici?** foomeh ee-see
swim here?	**nager ici?** nasheh ee-see
take photos here?	**prendre des photos ici?** prahnd deh photo ee-see
telephone here?	**téléphoner ici?** telephoneh ee-see
wait here?	**attendre ici?** attahnd ee-see

LIKELY REACTIONS

Yes, certainly	**Certainement** sairten-mahn
Help yourself	**Allez-y** alleh-zee
I think so	**Je crois** sher crwah
Or course	**Bien sûr** bee-an soor
Yes, but be careful	**Oui, mais faites attention** wee meh fet attahn-see-on
No, certainly not	**Certainement pas** sairten-mahn pah
I don't think so	**Je ne crois pas** sher ner crwah pah
Not normally	**Normalement, non** normahl-mahn non
Sorry	**Je regrette** sher rer-gret

Reference

PUBLIC NOTICES

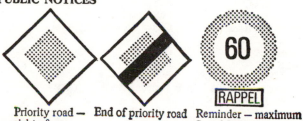

Priority road — End of priority road Reminder — maximum
right of way   Speed Limit

● Key words on signs for drivers, pedestrians, travellers, shoppers and overnight guests.

ACCOTEMENTS NON STABILISÉS	Soft shoulders
ALLUMEZ VOS PHARES	Lights on
A LOUER	To let
APPUYER ICI	Press here
ARRIVÉES	Arrivals
ASCENSEUR	Elevator
ATTENDEZ	Wait
ATTENTION	Caution
ATTENTION – CHIEN MÉCHANT	Beware of the dog
ATTENTION AUX TRAINS	Beware of the trains
AUTOROUTE	Highway
A VENDRE	For sale
BAIGNADE INTERDITE	No swimming
BIÈRE PRESSION	Draught beer
BILLETS	Tickets
BROCANTE	Antique/second-hand/junk shop
CAISSE	Cash desk
CAMPING INTERDIT	No camping
CENTRE VILLE	Town centre
CHAMBRE À LOUER	Room to rent
CHAMBRES LIBRES	Vacancies
CHAUD	Hot (tap)
CHAUSSÉE DÉFONCÉE	Bad surface (road)

CHAUSSÉE GLISSANTE	Slippery surface (road)
CHAUSSÉE RÉTRÉCIE	Road narrows
CHUTE DE PIERRES	Falling stones
CIRCUIT TOURISTIQUE	Scenic route
CLÉ MINUTE	Key cutting
COMPLET	Full – no vacancies
CONGÉ ANNUEL	Closed for holiday period
CONSIGNE	Left luggage
CYCLISTES	Bicycles
DAMES	Ladies
DÉFENSE D'AFFICHER	Bill posters will be prosecuted
DÉFENSE D'ENTRER SOUS PEINE D'AMENDE	Trespassers will be prosecuted
DÉPANNAGE	Emergency repairs
DÉPARTS	Departures
DÉVIATION	Detour
DOUCHE	Shower
EAU NON POTABLE	Not for drinking (water)
EAU POTABLE	Drinking water
ÉCOLE	School
EMPRUNTEZ LE SOUTERRAIN	Take the subway
EN RÉCLAME	Special offer
ENTRÉE	Entrance
ENTRÉE GRATUITE	Free entry
ENTRÉE INTERDITE	No entry
ESCALIER	Stairs
ÉTAGE (PREMIER, DEUXIÈME)	Floor (first, second)
FEMMES	Ladies
FERMÉ (LE LUNDI)	Closed (on Mondays)
FERMETURE ANNUELLE	Closed for holidays
FEUX DE CIRCULATION	Traffic lights
FILE DE DROITE	Right hand lane
FILE DE GAUCHE	Left hand lane
FIN D'AUTOROUTE	End of motorway
FRAPPEZ	Knock
FROID	Cold (tap)
GARE ROUTIÈRE	Coach station
GARE SNCF	Railway station
GRATUIT	Free
HÔPITAL	Hospital
IL EST INTERDIT DE DOUBLER	No passing

IL EST INTERDIT DE FUMER	No smoking
IMPASSE	Dead end
INTERDIT	Forbidden
INTERDIT AUX PIÉTONS	No pedestrians
INTRODUISEZ VOTRE PIÈCE ICI	Insert coin here
JOUR DE FERMETURE	Closing day
LAVABOS	Washbasins/Toilets
LAVERIE AUTOMATIQUE	Launderette
LIBRE	Free
LOCATION (DE VOITURES)	(Car) Hire
LOCATIONS	Bookings
MESSIEURS	Gentlemen
MÉTRO	Underground train
NETTOYAGE À SEC, PRESSING	Dry cleaning
OBJETS TROUVÉS	Lost property
OCCASIONS	Bargains
OCCUPÉ	Occupied
OUVERT	Open
PARKING	Car park
PARLER ICI	Speak here
PASSAGE À NIVEAU	Level crossing
PASSAGE SOUTERRAIN	Subway
PAYEZ À LA SORTIE	Pay on your way out
PAYEZ ICI	Pay here
PÉAGE	Toll
PIÉTONS	Pedestrians
PLACES DEBOUT	Standing room
POIDS LOURDS	Heavy goods vehicles
PORTEUR	Porter
POUSSEZ	Push
PRIÈRE DE NE PAS (TOUCHER)	Please do not (touch)
PRIORITÉ À DROITE	Priority to the right
PRIVÉ	Private
PROPRIÉTÉ PRIVÉE	Private property
QUAI	Platform/Quay
RALENTIR	Slow down
RELÂCHE	Closed (for theatres, cinemas)
REMISES	Reductions
RENSEIGNEMENTS	Information

RÉSERVÉ AUX AUTOBUS	Buses only
RÉSERVÉ AUX CYCLISTES	Bike lane
RESPECTEZ LES PELOUSES	Keep off the grass
REZ-DE-CHAUSSÉE	Ground floor
SABLES MOUVANTS	Quicksands
SALLE À MANGER	Dining room
SALLE D'ATTENTE	Waiting room
SENS UNIQUE	One way street
SERREZ À DROITE	Keep right
SOLDES	Sales
SONNEZ	Ring
SORTIE	Exit
SORTIE D'AUTOROUTE	Motorway exit
SORTIE DE CAMIONS	Truck exit – Caution
SORTIE DE SECOURS	Emergency exit
SOUS-SOL	Basement
STATIONNEMENT INTERDIT	No waiting
STATIONNEMENT JOURS IMPAIRS	Parking allowed on odd days of the month (1st, 3rd, 5th . . .)
STATIONNEMENT JOURS PAIRS	Parking allowed on even days of the month (2nd, 4th, 6th . . .)
STATIONNEMENT LIMITÉ	Restricted waiting
SYNDICAT D'INITIATIVE	Tourist information office
TERRAIN MILITAIRE	Military zone
TIREZ	Pull
TOURNEZ LA POIGNÉE	Turn the handle
TOUTES DIRECTIONS	Through traffic
TRAVAUX	Works
TRAVERSEZ	Cross
TVA EN SUS	Plus VAT
VENTES	Sales
VIRAGES	Bends
VITESSE LIMITÉE	Speed limit
VOIE	Platform
VOIE SANS ISSUE	No through road
ZONE BLEUE	Parking discs required
ZONE PIÉTONNIÈRE	Pedestrian precinct

ABBREVIATIONS

A	**autoroute**	highway
AJ	**Auberge de jeunesse**	Youth hostel
arr.	**arrondissement**	administrative district
CFF	**Chemins de Fer Fédéraux**	Swiss rail
ch.-l	**chef-lieu**	principal town in district
cl	**centilitre**	centilitre
D	**(route) départementale**	secondary road
dep.	**département**	administrative county
douz.	**douzaine**	dozen
EGDF	**Électricité et Gaz de France**	French Electricity and Gas
E.U.	**États-Unis**	United States
F	**fermé/franc/froid**	off/franc/cold
faub.	**faubourg**	suburb
FB	**Franc belge**	Belgian franc
FF	**Franc français**	French franc
FFCC	**Fédération Française de Camping et de Caravanning**	French Federation of Camping and Caravanning
FS	**Franc suisse**	Swiss franc
HT	**haute tension**	high voltage
K/Kg(s)	**kilogramme(s)**	kilogram(s)
Km	**kilomètre**	kilometre
L	**Livre sterling**	pound sterling
l	**litre**	litre
M/MM	**Monsieur/Messieurs**	Mr/Messrs
Mlle/Mlles	**Mademoiselle/Mesdemoiselles**	Miss/the Misses
Mme/Mmes	**Madame/Mesdames**	Mrs/Mesdames
N	**(route) nationale**	main highway
O	**Ouvert**	On
PT	**Postes et Télécommunications**	the Post Office
RD	**Route départementale**	secondary road
RER	**Réseau express régional**	express trains
RF	**République française**	French Republic
RN	**Route nationale**	main road
SI	**Syndicat d'initiative**	Tourist information office
SNCB	**Société Nationale des Chemins de Fer Belges**	Belgian Rail

SNCF	Société Nationale des Chemins de Fer Français	French Rail
s.pref.	sous-préfecture	important town in a 'département'
SS	Sécurité Sociale	Social Security/ National Health
THT	Très haute tension	Very high voltage
TSVP	Tournez s'il vous plaît	Please turn over
t.t.c.	toutes taxes comprises	tax inclusive
TVA	Taxe à la valeur ajoutée	value added tax (VAT)

NUMBERS

Cardinal numbers

0	zéro	zehro
1	un	an
2	deux	der
3	trois	trwah
4	quatre	kat
5	cinq	sank
6	six	seess
7	sept	set
8	huit	weet
9	neuf	nerf
10	dix	deess
11	onze	onz
12	douze	dooz
13	treize	trez
14	quatorze	kattorz
15	quinze	kanz
16	seize	sez
17	dix-sept	dee-set
18	dix-huit	deezweet
19	dix-neuf	deez-nerf
20	vingt	van
21	vingt et un	vanteh an
22	vingt-deux	vant-der
23	vingt-trois	vant-trwah
24	vingt-quatre	vant-kat
25	vingt-cinq	vant-sank

26	vingt-six	vant-seess
27	vingt-sept	vant-set
28	vingt-huit	vant-weet
29	vingt-neuf	vant-nerf
30	trente	trahnt
31	trente et un	trahnteh an
35	trente-cinq	trahnt sank
38	trente-huit	trahnt weet
40	quarante	kah-rahnt
41	quarante et un	kahrahnteh an
45	quarante-cinq	kah-rahnt sank
48	quarante-huit	kah-rahnt weet
50	cinquante	sankahnt
55	cinquante-cinq	sankahnt sank
60	soixante	swah-sahnt
65	soixante-cinq	swah-sahnt sank
70	soixante-dix	swah-sahnt deess
75	soixante-quinze	swah-sahnt kanz
80	quatre-vingts	kat van
85	quatre-vingt-cinq	kat van sank
90	quatre-vingt-dix	kat van deess
95	quatre-vingt-quinze	kat van kanz
100	cent	sahn
101	cent un	sahn an
102	cent deux	sahn der
125	cent vingt-cinq	sahn vant sank
150	cent cinquante	sahn sankahnt
175	cent soixante-quinze	sahn swah-sahnt kanz
200	deux cents	der sahn
300	trois cents	trwah sahn
400	quatre cents	kat sahn
500	cinq cents	san sahn
1,000	mille	meel
1,500	mille cinq cents	meel san sahn
2,000	deux mille	der meel
5,000	cinq mille	san meel
10,000	dix mille	dee meel
100,000	cent mille	sahn meel
1,000,000	un million	an meel-yon

Ordinal numbers

1st	premier (1e)	prem-yeh
2nd	deuxième (2e)	derz-yem
3rd	troisième (3e)	trwahz-yem
4th	quatrième (4e)	katr-yem
5th	cinquième (5e)	sank-yem
6th	sixième (6c)	seess-yem
7th	septième (7e)	set-yem
8th	huitième (8e)	weet-yem
9th	neuvième (9e)	nerf-yem
10th	dixième (10e)	deess-yem
11th	onzième (11⁻)	onz-yem
12th	douzième (12e)	dooz-yem

TIME

What time is it?	**Quelle heure est-il?**
	keller eh-til
It's one o'clock	**Il est une heure**
	il eh ooner
It's ...	**Il est ...**
	il eh ...
two o'clock	**deux heures**
	der-zer
three o'clock	**trois heures**
	trwah-zer
four o'clock	**quatre heures**
	kat-er
in the morning	**du matin**
	doo mahtan
in the afternoon	**de l'après-midi**
	der lahpreh meedee
in the evening	**du soir**
	doo swah
It's ...	**Il est ...**
	il eh ...
noon	**midi**
	meedee
midnight	**minuit**
	meenwee

It's ...	Il est ... il eh ...
five past five	**cinq heures cinq** sanker sank
ten past five	**cinq heures dix** sanker deess
a quarter past five	**cinq heures et quart** sanker eh kar
twenty past five	**cinq heures vingt** sanker van
twenty-five past five	**cinq heures vingt-cinq** sanker vant sank
half past five	**cinq heures et demie** sanker eh der-me
twenty-five to six	**six heures moins vingt-cinq** seezer mwen vant sank
twenty to six	**six heures moins vingt** seezer mwen van
a quarter to six	**six heures moins le quart** seezer mwen ler kar
ten to six	**six heures moins dix** seezer mwen deess
five to six	**six heures moins cinq** seezer mwen sank
At what time ... (does the train leave)? At ...	**A quelle heure ... (part le train)?** ah keller ... (par ler tran) **A ...** ah ...
13.00	**treize heures** trez-er
14.05	**quatorze heures zéro cinq** kattorzer zehro sank
15.10	**quinze heures dix** kanzer deess
16.15	**seize heures quinze** sez-er kanz
17.20	**dix-sept heures vingt** dee-set er van
18.25	**dix-huit heures vingt-cinq** deezweet er vant sank
19.30	**dix-neuf heures trente** deez nerv-er trahnt

At...	A... ah ...
20.35	**vingt heures trente-cinq** vant-er trahnt sank
21.40	**vingt et une heures quarante** vant eh ooner kah-rahnt
22.45	**vingt-deux heures quarante-cinq** vant der zer kah-rahnt sank
23.50	**vingt-trois heures cinquante** vant trwah zer sankahnt
0.55	**zéro heure cinquante-cinq** zehro er sankahnt sank
in ten minutes	**dans dix minutes** dahn dee meenoot
in a quarter of an hour	**dans un quart d'heure** dahn-zan kar der
in half an hour	**dans une demi-heure** dahn-zoon der-me-er
in three quarters of an hour	**dans trois quarts d'heure** dahn trwah kar der

DAYS

Monday	**lundi** lerndee
Tuesday	**mardi** mardee
Wednesday	**mercredi** mairk-dee
Thursday	**jeudi** sher-dee
Friday	**vendredi** vahnd-dee
Saturday	**samedi** samdee
Sunday	**dimanche** deemahnsh
last Monday	**lundi dernier** lerndee dairn-yeh
next Tuesday	**mardi prochain** mardee proshan

on Wednesday	**mercredi**
	mairk-dee
on Thursdays	**le jeudi**
	ler sher-dee
until Friday	**jusqu'à vendredi**
	shooskah vahnd-dee
before Saturday	**avant samedi**
	ahvahn samdee
after Sunday	**après dimanche**
	ahpreh deemahnsh
the day before yesterday	**avant-hier**
	ahvahntee-air
two days ago	**il y a deux jours**
	il yah der shoor
yesterday	**hier**
	ee-air
yesterday morning	**hier matin**
	ee-air mahtan
yesterday afternoon	**hier après-midi**
	ee-air ahpreh-meedee
last night (evening)	**hier soir**
	ee-air swah
today	**aujourd' hui**
	o-shoordwee
this morning	**ce matin**
	ser mahtan
this afternoon	**cet après-midi**
	set ahpreh meedee
tonight	**ce soir**
	ser swah
tomorrow	**demain**
	der-man
tomorrow morning	**demain matin**
	der-man mahtan
tomorrow afternoon	**demain après-midi**
	der-man ahpreh meedee
tomorrow evening] tomorrow night	**demain soir**
	der-man swah
the day after tomorrow	**après-demain**
	ahpreh der-man

MONTHS AND DATES

January	janvier
	shahnv-yeh
February	février
	fehvree-eh
March	mars
	marss
April	avril
	avreel
May	mai
	meh
June	juin
	shoo-an
July	juillet
	shwee-yeh
August	août
	oot
September	septembre
	septahmb
October	octobre
	octob
November	novembre
	novahmb
December	décembre
	dessahmb
in January	au mois de janvier
	o mwah der shahnv-yeh
until February	jusqu'au mois de février
	shoosko mwah der fehvree-eh
before March	avant le mois de mars
	ahvahn ler mwah der marss
after April	après le mois d'avril
	ahpreh ler mwah davreel
during May	pendant le mois de mai
	pahndahn ler mwah der meh
not until June	pas avant le mois de juin
	pah ahvahn ler mwah der shoo-an
the beginning of July	le début juillet
	ler dehboo shwee-yeh
the middle of August	la mi-août
	lah me-oot

the end of September	**la fin septembre**
	lah fan septahmb
last month	**le mois dernier**
	ler mwah dairn-yeh
this month	**ce mois-ci**
	ser mwah-see
next month	**le mois prochain**
	ler mwah proshan
in spring	**au printemps**
	o prantahn
in summer	**en été**
	ahn eh-teh
in autumn	**en automne**
	ahn oton
in winter	**en hiver**
	ahn eevair
this year	**cette année**
	set anneh
last year	**l'année dernière**
	lanneh dairn-yair
next year	**l'année prochaine**
	lanneh proshen
in 1982	**en mil neuf cent quatre-vingt-deux**
	ahn mil nerf sahn kat van der
in 1985	**en mil neuf cent quatre-vingt-cinq**
	ahn mil nerf sahn kat van sank
in 1990	**en mil neuf cent quatre-vingt-dix**
	ahn mil nerf sahn kat van deess
What's the date today?	**Quel jour sommes-nous?**
	kel shoor som noo
It's the 6th of March	**C'est le six mars**
	seh ler see marss
It's the 12th of April	**C'est le douze avril**
	seh ler dooz avreel
It's the 21st of August	**C'est le vingt et un août**
	seh le vanteh an oot

Public holidays in France and Belgium
● On these days, offices, shops and schools are closed.

1 January	Jour de l'An	New Year's Day
...	Lundi de Pâques	Easter Monday
1 May	Fête du Travail	Labour Day
...	Ascension	Ascension Day
...	Lundi de Pentecôte	Whit Monday
14 July	Quatorze Juillet	Bastille Day (France)
21 July	Fête Nationale	National Day (Belgium)
15 August	Assomption	Assumption Day
	Quinze Août	
1 November	Toussaint	All Saints Day
11 November	Armistice	Remembrance Day
25 December	Noël	Christmas Day
26 December	Saint-Étienne	St Stephen's Day (Belgium)

COUNTRIES AND NATIONALITIES

Countries

Australia	(l') Australie
	(l) ostrah-lee
Austria	(l') Autriche
	(l) otreesh
Belgium	(la) Belgique
	(lah) belsheek
Britain	(la) Grande-Bretagne
	(lah) grahnd brer-tan
Canada	(le) Canada
	(ler) canadah
East Africa	(l') Afrique de l'Est
	(l) ahfreek der lest
Eire	(l') Irlande du Sud
	(l) eerlahnd doo sood
England	(l') Angleterre
	(l) ahng-tair
France	(la) France
	(lah) frahns
Greece	(la) Grèce
	(lah) gress
India	(l') Inde
	(l) and

Italy	(l') Italie
	(l) eetah-lee
Luxembourg	(le) Luxembourg
	(ler) look-sahn-boor
Netherlands	(la) Hollande
	(lah) ollahnd
New Zealand	(la) Nouvelle-Zélande
	(lah) noovel zehlahnd
Northern Ireland	(l') Irlande du Nord
	(l) eerlahnd doo nor
Pakistan	(le) Pakistan
	(ler) pakistan
Portugal	(le) Portugal
	(ler) portoogal
Scotland	(l') Écosse
	(l) ehcoss
South Africa	(l') Afrique du Sud
	(l) ahfreek doo sood
Spain	(l') Espagne
	(l) espan
Switzerland	(la) Suisse
	(lah) sweess
United States	(les) États-Unis
	(leh-z) ehtah-zoonee
Wales	(le) Pays de Galles
	(ler) peh-ee der gal
West Germany	(l') Allemagne de l'Ouest
	(l) alman der loo-est
West Indies	(les) Antilles
	(leh-z) ahntee
in England	en Angleterre
	ahn ahng-tair
in Switzerland	en Suisse
	ahn sweess
in Pakistan	au Pakistan
	o pakistan
in Portugal	au Portugal
	o portoogal
in the United States	aux États-Unis
	o-zehtah-zoonee
in the West Indies	aux Antilles
	o-zahntee

Nationalities
[Use the first alternative for men, the second for women.]

American	**américain/américaine** american/ameriken
Australian	**australien/australienne** ostrahl-yan/ostrahl-yen
British	**britannique** britanneek
Canadian	**canadien/canadienne** canahdee-an/canahdee-en
East African	**est-africain/est-africaine** est-african/est-afriken
English	**anglais/anglaise** ahngleh/ahnglez
Indian	**indien/indienne** andee-an/andee-en
Irish	**irlandais/irlandaise** eerlahndeh/eerlahndez
a New Zealander	**néo-zélandais/néo-zélandaise** nay-o-zehlahn-deh/nay-o- zehlahndez
a Pakistani	**pakistanais/pakistanaise** pakistan-eh/pakistan-ez
Scots	**écossais/écossaise** eh-cosseh/eh-cossez
South African	**sud-africain/sud-africaine** sood-african/sood-afriken
Welsh	**gallois/galloise** gahlwah/gahlwaz
West Indian	**antillais/antillaise** ahntee-yeh/ahntee-yez

DEPARTMENT STORE GUIDE

Accessoires automobile	Car accessories
Accessoires cuisine	Kitchen gadgets
Accessoires mode	Fashion accessories
Alimentation	Food
Ameublement	Soft Furnishings
Articles de mode	Fashion articles
Articles de voyage	Travel articles
Arts ménagers	China, glassware, kitchenware
Bas	Stockings
Bijouterie	Jewellery
Blanc	Household linen
Bricolage	Do-it-yourself
Cadeaux	Gifts
Caisse	Cash desk
Camping	Camping
Ceintures	Belts
Chemiserie	Shirts
Chemises	Shirts
Chaussures	Shoes
Confection	Ready-to-wear
Coussins	Cushions
Couvertures	Blankets
Cravates	Ties
Crédits	Credit-Accounts
Dame(s)	Woman/women's wear
Deuxième	Second
Disques	Records
Éclairage	Lighting
Électro-ménager	Electrical appliances
Enfant(s)	Child/children
Entretien	Cleaning materials
Étage	Floor
Gaines	Girdles
Homme(s)	Man/men's wear
Jouets	Toys
Layette	Babywear
Librairie	Books
Linge maison	Household linen
Lingerie	Women's underwear
Literie	Bedding

Maquillage	Make-up
Maroquinerie	Leather goods
Mercerie	Haberdashery
Meubles	Furniture
Meubles de cuisine	Kitchen furniture
Mode(s)	Fashions
Pantoufles	Slippers
Papèterie	Stationery
Parfumerie	Perfumery
Photo(graphie)	Photography
Premier	First
Prêt-à-porter	Ready-to-wear
Produits de beauté	Beauty products
Pulls	Jumpers
Quatrième	Fourth
Quincaillerie	Hardware
Radio	Radio
Renseignements	Information
Revêtements de sol	Floor coverings
Rez-de-chaussée	Ground floor
Rideaux	Curtains
Service après-vente	Complaints, repairs
Sous-sol	Basement
Sous-vêtements	Underwear
Soutiens-gorge	Bras
Talon minute	Heel bar
Tapis	Carpets
Télévision	Television
Tissus	Fabrics
Tissus d'ameublement	Furnishing fabrics
Troisième	Third
Vaisselle	China
Verrerie	Glassware

CONVERSION TABLES

Read the centre column of these tables from right to left to convert
from metric to imperial and from left to right to convert from
imperial to metric e.g. 5 litres = 8.80 pints; 5 pints = 2.84 litres.

pints		litres		gallons		litres
1.76	1	0.57		0.22	1	4.55
3.52	2	1.14		0.44	2	9.09
5.28	3	1.70		0.66	3	13.64
7.07	4	2.27		0.88	4	18.18
8.80	5	2.84		1.00	5	22.73
10.56	6	3.41		1.32	6	27.28
12.32	7	3.98		1.54	7	31.82
14.08	8	4.55		1.76	8	36.37
15.84	9	5.11		1.98	9	40.91

ounces		grams		pounds		kilos
0.04	1	28.35		2.20	1	0.45
0.07	2	56.70		4.41	2	0.91
0.11	3	85.05		6.61	3	1.36
0.14	4	113.40		8.82	4	1.81
0.18	5	141.75		11.02	5	2.27
0.21	6	170.10		13.23	6	2.72
0.25	7	198.45		15.43	7	3.18
0.28	8	226.80		17.64	8	3.63
0.32	9	255.15		19.84	9	4.08

inches		centimetres		yards		metres
0.39	1	2.54		1.09	1	0.91
0.79	2	5.08		2.19	2	1.83
1.18	3	7.62		3.28	3	2.74
1.58	4	10.16		4.37	4	3.66
1.95	5	12.70		5.47	5	4.57
2.36	6	15.24		6.56	6	5.49
2.76	7	17.78		7.66	7	6.40
3.15	8	20.32		8.65	8	7.32
3.54	9	22.86		9.84	9	8.23

miles		kilometres
0.62	1	1.61
1.24	2	3.22
1.86	3	4.83
2.49	4	6.44
3.11	5	8.05
3.73	6	9.66
4.35	7	11.27
4.97	8	12.87
5.59	9	14.48

A quick way to convert kilometres to miles: divide by 8 and multiply by 5. To convert miles to kilometres: divide by 5 and multiply by 8.

fahrenheit (°F)	centigrade (°C)	lbs/ sq in	k/ sq cm
212°	100° boiling point	18	1.3
100°	38°	20	1.4
98.4°	36.9° body temperature	22	1.5
86°	30°	25	1.7
77°	25°	29	2.0
68°	20°	32	2.3
59°	15°	35	2.5
50°	10°	36	2.5
41°	5°	39	2.7
32°	0° freezing point	40	2.8
14°	−10°	43	3.0
−4°	−20°	45	3.2
		46	3.2
		50	3.5
		60	4.2

To convert °C to °F: divide by 5, multiply by 9 and add 32. To convert °F to °C: subtract 32, divide by 9 and multiply by 5.

CLOTHING SIZES

Remember – always try on clothes before buying. Clothing sizes are usually unreliable.

women's dresses and suits

Europe	38	40	42	44	46	48
UK	32	34	36	38	40	42
USA	10	12	14	16	18	20

men's suits and coats

Europe	46	48	50	52	54	56
UK and USA	36	38	40	42	44	46

men's shirts

Europe	36	37	38	39	41	42	43
UK and USA	14	$14\frac{1}{2}$	15	$15\frac{1}{2}$	16	$16\frac{1}{2}$	17

socks

Europe	38–39	39–40	40–41	41–42	42–43
UK and USA	$9\frac{1}{2}$	10	$10\frac{1}{2}$	11	$11\frac{1}{2}$

shoes

Europe	34	$35\frac{1}{2}$	$36\frac{1}{2}$	38	39	41	42	43	44	45
UK	2	3	4	5	6	7	8	9	10	11
USA	$3\frac{1}{2}$	$4\frac{1}{2}$	$5\frac{1}{2}$	$6\frac{1}{2}$	$7\frac{1}{2}$	$8\frac{1}{2}$	$9\frac{1}{2}$	$10\frac{1}{2}$	$11\frac{1}{2}$	$12\frac{1}{2}$

Do it yourself

Some notes on the language

This section does not deal with 'grammar' as such. The purpose here is to explain some of the most obvious and elementary nuts and bolts of the language, based on the principal phrases included in the book. This information should enable you to produce numerous sentences of your own making.

There is no pronunciation guide in the first section, partly because it would get in the way of the explanations and partly because you have to do it yourself at this stage if you are serious – work out the pronunciation from all the earlier examples in the book.

THE

All nouns in French belong to one of two genders: masculine or feminine, irrespective of whether they refer to living beings or inanimate objects.

The	masculine	feminine	plural	
the address		l'adresse	les adresses	the addresses
the apple		la pomme	les pommes	the apples
the bill		l'addition	les additions	the bills
the cup of tea		la tasse de thé	les tasses de thé	the cups of tea
the glass of beer	le verre de bière		les verres de bière	the glasses of beer
the key		la clé	les clés	the keys
the luggage			les bagages	the luggage
the menu	le menu		les menus	the menus
the newspaper	le journal		les journaux	the newspapers
the receipt	le reçu		les reçus	the receipts
the sandwich	le sandwich		les sandwichs	the sandwiches
the suitcase		la valise	les valises	the suitcases
the telephone directory	l'annuaire téléphonique		les annuaires téléphoniques	the telephone directories
the timetable	l'horaire		les horaires	the timetables

Important things to remember

● *The* is le before a masculine noun, and la before a feminine noun.
● *The* is l' before masculine and feminine nouns which begin with a

vowel (*h* often counts as a vowel): **l'adresse** (f) and **l'horaire** (m), when referring to a single thing.

● There is no way of predicting whether a noun is masculine **or** feminine. You have to learn and remember its gender. Obviously, if you are reading a word with le or la in front of it, you can detect its gender immediately: **le menu** is masculine (*m.* in dictionaries) and **la valise** is feminine (*f.* in dictionaries).

● Does it matter? Not unless you want to make a serious attempt to speak correctly and scratch beneath the surface of the language. You would be understood if you said **la menu**, or even **le horaire**, provided your pronunciation was good.

● *The* is always **les** before a noun in the plural.

● As a general rule, a noun adds an 's' to become plural, but this does not change its pronunciation: **clé** and **clés** sound the same. But watch out for many exceptions such as **journal/journaux**.

● In French, luggage is always regarded as plural. It is never used to mean a single item.

Practise saying and writing these sentences in French:

Have you got the key?	**Avez-vous la clé?**
Have you got the luggage?	**Avez-vous . . . ?**
Have you got the telephone directory?	
Have you got the menu?	
I'd like the key	**Je voudrais la clé**
I'd like the receipt	**Je voudrais . . .**
I'd like the bill	
I'd like the keys	
Where is the key?	**Où est la clé?**
Where is the timetable?	**Où est . . . ?**
Where is the address?	
Where is the suitcase?	
Where are the keys?	**Où sont les clés?**
Where are the sandwiches?	**Où sont . . . ?**
Where are the apples?	
Where are the suitcases?	
Where is the luggage?	**Où sont . . . ?**
Where can I get the key?	**Où puis-je trouver la clé?**
Where can I get the address?	**Où puis-je trouver . . . ?**
Where can I get the timetables?	

Now make up more sentences along the same lines. Try adding *please*: **s'il vous plaît**, at the end.

A/AN

A/an	masculine	feminine	plural	some/any
an address		une adresse	des adresses	addresses
an apple		une pomme	des pommes	apples
a bill		une addition	des additions	bills
a cup of tea		une tasse de thé	des tasses de thé	cups of tea
a glass of beer	un verre de bière		des verres de bière	glasses of beer
a key		une clé	des clés	keys
...	...	...	des bagages	luggage
a menu	un menu		des menus	menus
a newspaper	un journal		des journaux	newspapers
a receipt	un reçu		des reçus	receipts
a sandwich	un sandwich		des sandwichs	sandwiches
a suitcase		une valise	des valise	suitcases
a telephone directory	un annuaire téléphonique		des annuaires téléphoniques	telephone directories
a timetable	un horaire		des horaires	timetables

Important things to remember

● *A* or *an* is always un before a masculine noun, and une before a feminine noun.
● *Some* or *any* is always des before a noun in the plural. In certain expressions in French, des is left out: see an example of this in the sentences marked with a * below.

Practise saying and writing these sentences in French:

Have you got a receipt?	Avez-vous ... ?
Have you got a menu?	
I'd like a telephone directory	Je voudrais ...
I'd like some sandwiches	
Where can I get some newspapers?	Où puis-je trouver ... ?
Where can I get a cup of tea?	
Is there a key?	Est-ce qu'il y a une clé?
Is there a timetable?	Est-ce qu'il y a ... ?
Is there a telephone directory?	
Is there a menu?	
Are there any keys?	Est-ce qu'il y a des clés?
Are there any newspapers?	Est-ce qu'il y a ... ?
Are there any sandwiches?	

Now make up more sentences along the same lines.

Then try these new phrases:
Je vais prendre ... (I'll have ...)
J'ai besoin de ... (I need ...)

I'll have a glass of beer	Je vais prendre un verre de bière
I'll have a cup of tea	Je vais prendre ...
I'll have some sandwiches	
I'll have some apples	
I need a cup of tea	J'ai besoin d'une tasse de thé
I need a key	J'ai besoin d' ...
*I need some newspapers	J'ai besoin de journaux
*I need some keys	J'ai besoin de ...
*I need some addresses	J'ai besoin d' ...
*I need some sandwiches	
*I need some suitcases	

SOME/ANY

In cases where some or any refer to more than one thing, such as *some/any ice-creams* and *some/any tomatoes*, the word **des** is used as explained earlier:

des glaces	some/any ice-creams
des tomates	some/any tomatoes

As a guide, you can usually *count* the number of containers or whole items.
In cases where *some* refers to part of a whole thing or an indefinite quantity, the word **des** cannot be used.
Look at the list below:

the bread	le pain	du pain	some bread
the ice-cream	la glace	de la glace	some ice-cream
the pineapple	l'ananas (m)	de l'ananas	some pineapple
the tomato	la tomate	de la tomate	some tomato
the water	l'eau (f)	de l'eau	some water
the wine	le vin	du vin	some wine

Important things to remember

● **Du** is used for masculine nouns.
● **De la** is used for feminine nouns.
● **De l'** is used for both masculine and feminine nouns which begin with a vowel.

Can you complete the list below?

the aspirin	l'aspirine (f)	. . . some aspirin
the beer	la bière	. . . some beer
the cheese	le fromage	. . . some cheese
the coffee	le café	. . . some coffee
the lemonade	la limonade	. . . some lemonade
the tea	le thé	. . . some tea

Practise saying and writing these sentences in French:

Have you got some coffee?	Avez vous du café?
Have you got some ice-cream?	
Have you got some pineapple?	
I'd like some aspirin	Je voudrais de l'aspirine
I'd like some tomato	
I'd like some bread	
Is there any lemonade?	Est-ce qu'il y a de la limonade?
Is there any water?	
Is there any wine?	
Where can I get some cheese?	Où puis-je trouver du fromage?
Where can I get some ice-cream?	
Where can I get some water?	
I'll have some beer	Je vais prendre de la bière
I'll have some tea	
I'll have some coffee	

THIS AND THAT

One word in French: ça
If you don't know the French name for an object, just point and say:

Je voudrais ça	I'd like that
Je vais prendre ça	I'll have that
J'ai besoin de ça	I need this

HELPING OTHERS

You can help yourself with phrases such as:

I'd like . . . a sandwich	Je voudrais . . . un sandwich
Where can I get . . . a cup of tea?	Où puis-je trouver . . . une tasse de thé?
I'll have . . . a glass of beer	Je vais prendre . . . un verre de bière
I need . . . a receipt	J'ai besoin d' . . . une facture

If you come across a compatriot having trouble making himself understood, you should be able to speak to the French person on their behalf.

He'd like . . .	Il voudrait un sandwich
	il voodreh an sandwich
She'd like . . .	Elle voudrait un sandwich
	el voodreh an sandwich
Where can he get . . . ?	Où peut-il trouver une tasse de thé?
	oo per til trooveh oon tass der teh
Where can she get . . . ?	Où peut-elle trouver une tasse de thé?
	oo per tel trooveh oon tass der teh
He'll have . . .	Il va prendre un verre de bière
	il vah prahnd an vair der be-air
She'll have . . .	Elle va prendre un verre de bière
	el vah prahnd an vair der be-air
He needs . . .	Il a besoin d'un reçu
	il ah ber-zwan dan rer-soo
She needs . . .	Elle a besoin d'un reçu
	el ah ber-zwan dan rer-soo

You can also help a couple or a group if *they* are having difficulties. There are two French words for *they*: elles (women) and ils (men). When women and men are mixed, *they* are referred to as ils. If *they* are a married couple, for example, the word is ils.

They'd like . . .	Ils voudraient du fromage
	il voodreh doo fromash
	Elles voudraient du fromage
	el voodreh doo fromash
Where can they get . . . ?	Où peuvent-ils trouver de l'aspirine?
	oo perv til trooveh der laspeereen
	Où peuvent-elles trouver de l'aspirine?
	oo perv tel trooveh der laspeereen

They'll have ...	**Ils vont prendre du vin**
	il von prahnd doo van
	Elles vont prendre du vin
	el von prahnd doo van
They need ...	**Ils ont besoin d'eau**
	il zon ber-zwan do
	Elles ont besoin d'eau
	el zon ber-zwan do

What about the two of you? No problem. The word for *we* is **nous**.

We'd like ...	**Nous voudrions du vin**
	noo voodree-on doo van
Where can we get ... ?	**Où pouvons-nous trouver de l'eau?**
	oo poovon noo trooveh der lo
We'll have ...	**Nous allons prendre de la bière**
	noo ahlon prahnd der lah be-air
We need ...	**Nous avons besoin d'aspirine**
	noo zahvon ber-zwan daspeereen

Try writing out your own checklists for these four useful phrase-starters, like this:

Je voudrais ...	**Nous voudrions ...**
Il voudrait ...	**Ils voudraient ...**
Elle voudrait ...	**Elles voudraient ...**
Où puis-je trouver ... ?	**Où ... -nous trouver ... ?**
Où peut-il trouver ... ?	**Où ... -ils trouver ... ?**
Où peut-elle trouver ... ?	**Où ... -elles trouver ... ?**

MORE PRACTICE

Here are some more French names of things. See how many different
sentences you can make up, using the various points of information
given earlier in this section.

		singular	plural
1	ashtray	cendrier (m)	cendriers
2	bag	sac (m)	sacs
3	broom	balai (m)	balais
4	car	voiture (f)	voitures
5	cigarette	cigarette (f)	cigarettes
6	corkscrew	tire-bouchon (m)	tire-bouchons
7	glove	gant (m)	gants
8	ice-cream	glace (f)	glaces
9	melon	melon (m)	melons
10	passport	passeport (m)	passeports
11	rag (dish cloth)	torchon (m)	torchons
12	salad	salade (f)	salades
13	saucepan	casserole (f)	casseroles
14	shoe	chaussure (f)	chaussures
15	stamp	timbre (m)	timbres
16	station	gare (f)	gares
17	street	rue (f)	rues
18	sunglasses		lunettes de soleil (f)
19	telephone	téléphone (m)	téléphones
20	ticket	billet (m)	billets

Index

Regions

U.K

Calais
Boulogne
Belgium
Germany

NORD/PAS-
DE-CALAIS

Cherbourg

PICARDY

NORMANDY
PARIS &
ILE DE
FRANCE
CHAMPAGNE
-ARDENNE
ALSACE
VOSGES-
LORRAINE

BRITTANY

WESTERN
LOIRE
LOIRE VALLEY
(CENTRE)
BURGUNDY
FRANCHE-
COMTE

Switzerland

POITOU
CHARENTES

LIMOUSIN
Lyon
SAVOY &
DAUPHINY
ALPS

AUVERGNE

Italy

Bordeaux

AQUITAINE
RHONE
VALLEY

MIDI
-PYRENEES
LANGUEDOC-
ROUSSILLON
PROVENCE
COTE
d'AZUR

Marseille

Spain

0 ___ km ___ 150

CORSICA

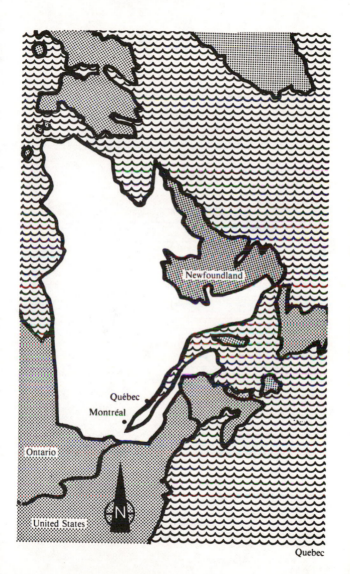

Newfoundland

Québec

Montréal

Ontario

United States

N

Quebec

Ostend
Bruges
Ghent
Brussels
Liège
Netherlands
Germany
Lux.
France
N
Belgium

France

W. Germany

Bâle

Zürich

Bienne

Berne

SWITZERLAND

Lausanne

Genève

Italy

N

French Switzerland

Notes

Notes

LANGUAGE AND TRAVEL BOOKS

Multilingual
The Insult Dictionary:
    How to Give 'Em Hell in 5 Nasty Languages
The Lover's Dictionary:
    How to be Amorous in 5 Delectable Languages
Multilingual Phrase Book
International Traveler's Phrasebook

Spanish
Vox Spanish and English Dictionaries
Harrap's Concise Spanish and English Dictionary
The Spanish Businessmate
Nice 'n Easy Spanish Grammar
Spanish Verbs and Essentials of Grammar
Getting Started in Spanish
Guide to Spanish Idioms
Guide to Correspondence in Spanish
Diccionario Básico Norteamericano

French
Harrap's French and English Dictionaries
French Verbs and Essentials of Grammar
Getting Started in French
Guide to French Idioms
Guide to Correspondence in French
The French Businessmate
Nice 'n Easy French Grammar

German
New Schöffler-Weis German and English Dictionary
Klett German and English Dictionary
Harrap's Concise German and English Dictionary
Getting Started in German
German Verbs and Essentials of Grammar
Guide to German Idioms
The German Businessmate
Nice 'n Easy German Grammar

Italian
Getting Started in Italian
Italian Verbs and Essentials of Grammar

Russian
Russian Essentials of Grammar
Business Russian

Japanese
Japanese in Plain English
Everyday Japanese

Just Enough Books
Just Enough Dutch
Just Enough French
Just Enough German
Just Enough Greek
Just Enough Italian
Just Enough Japanese
Just Enough Portuguese
Just Enough Scandinavian
Just Enough Serbo-Croat
Just Enough Spanish

Language Programs
Just Listen 'n Learn Spanish, French,
    German, Italian and Greek
Just Listen 'n Learn PLUS: in Spanish,
    French, German
Practice & Improve Your . . . Spanish, French
    and German
Practice & Improve Your . . . Spanish, French and
    German PLUS

Travel and Reference
Nagel's Encyclopedia Guides
World at Its Best Travel Series
Mystery Reader's Walking Guide: London
Business Capitals of the World
European Atlas
Health Guide for International Travelers
Passport's Japan Almanac
Passport's Travel Paks
Japan at Night
Japan Today
British/American Language Dictionary
Bon Voyage!
Hiking and Walking Guide to Europe

 PASSPORT BOOKS

a division of *NTC Publishing Group*
4255 West Touhy Avenue
Lincolnwood, Illinois 60646-1975